HYPERTENSION
COOKBOOK

HYPERTENSION
COOKBOOK

RECIPES

Karen A. Levin

PHOTOGRAPHS

Sheri Giblin

MEREDITH® BOOKS

Des Moines, Iowa

CONTENTS

EATING FOR BETTER HEALTH

ONE OUT OF TWO AMERICANS DEVELOPS HIGH BLOOD PRESSURE BY AGE SIXTY-FIVE. THE EXACT CAUSE OF HIGH BLOOD PRESSURE, WHICH DOCTORS CALL hypertension, is unknown, but there is much you can do to lower your risk of developing it or to keep it under control if you've been told you have it. Diet plays a key role. Salt has been blamed for raising blood pressure in many people, especially in people who are overweight. Weight gain from overeating is another risk factor. Heavy drinking can also lead to high blood pressure.

Because hypertension can damage the heart and blood vessels, it is beneficial to eat a heart-healthy diet that is moderate in calories, low in unhealthy saturated and trans fats, and rich in low-fat dairy products and high-fiber foods, especially vegetables, fruits, whole grains, and legumes. If you're overweight, losing as little as 5 or 10 pounds can lower your blood pressure.

Along with following your doctor's advice, adding dishes from the *American Medical Association Hypertension Cookbook* to your weekly menus can help you achieve and maintain healthy blood pressure. These sixty recipes, which are delicious and very easy to prepare, have been developed using guidelines established specifically to help you and your family fight hypertension.

UNDERSTANDING HYPERTENSION

High blood pressure is the most common chronic illness in the United States, affecting more than 65 million Americans, many of whom are unaware they have it. It is also the most frequent cause of stroke and a major risk factor for heart disease. The good news is that it can often be avoided, is easy to diagnose, and is usually easy to treat.

Disease-fighting foods: (facing page, clockwise from top left) mixed salad greens, broccoli florets, halibut fillets, and whole-grain bread.

The silent disease

Hypertension is often called "the silent killer" because it seldom causes symptoms in the early stages. By the time it produces symptoms—headaches, heart palpitations, and shortness of breath—it may already have caused organ damage. The condition was once deemed a disease of aging, but more and more children are developing it, mainly due to being overweight and inactive.

Hypertension's harmful effects

In hypertension, the blood puts excessive pressure on the walls of the blood vessels, making them stiffer and more prone to narrowing from a buildup of fatty deposits called plaque. The added pressure forces the heart to strain and grow larger, raising the risk of a heart attack or heart failure. The blood vessels that feed the brain can become blocked or can burst, causing a stroke. Less circulation to the kidneys can lead to kidney damage and kidney failure.

Know your numbers

Because uncontrolled hypertension is stealthy, you should have your blood pressure taken regularly throughout your life—ideally every time you visit the doctor. Blood pressure is noted in millimeters of mercury (mm Hg). The first number in a reading, called the systolic pressure, is the pressure as the heart beats; the second, lower number, called the diastolic pressure, is the pressure between beats. Here's what the numbers mean.

• **Healthy**—below *120/80 mm Hg*

• **Prehypertension**—(you are at high risk of developing hypertension) *120–139/80–89 mm Hg*

• **Hypertension**—*140/90 mm Hg or higher*

Many workplaces and pharmacies have automatic blood pressure machines available. If you have hypertension, your doctor may recommend purchasing a blood pressure machine to use at home.

CONTROLLING BLOOD PRESSURE

Hypertension has no cure but it is relatively easy to treat, usually with medication. At an early stage, some people can successfully lower their blood pressure by losing weight, eating a nutritious diet, and exercising regularly. Even if you take medication, a healthy lifestyle can improve your blood pressure and help you avoid life-threatening complications.

A healthy dinner, such as the one shown here, consists of a reasonable portion of protein with a heart-healthy green vegetable served alongside.

Outdoor activities (facing page) such as bicycling and brisk walking are fun and effective ways to keep weight down and hypertension under control.

Eat a healthy diet

A hypertension-fighting diet is heart healthy and calorie conscious; low in salt, added sugars, and harmful fats; and high in fiber and minerals. In particular, it is rich in vegetables, fruits, and low-fat dairy products; includes whole grains, fish, poultry, and nuts; and is low in saturated and trans fats, total fat, and cholesterol. A healthy diet also limits red meats, sweets, sugary drinks, alcohol, and sometimes caffeine.

Lose weight

If you are overweight, even a modest weight loss can reduce your risk of developing high blood pressure and can lower your blood pressure if you already have hypertension, possibly eliminating the need for medication. Avoid programs that abolish whole food groups such as carbohydrates—they can leave you dangerously short of essential nutrients. The key to losing weight is to burn more calories than you consume.

Stay active

Regular exercise improves the fitness of your heart, blood vessels, and lungs, helping to lower blood pressure and protect against heart disease. Heart-healthy exercises include walking, swimming, and stair climbing. For the most benefit, exercise for 30 to 60 minutes a day.

Cut down on salt

Excess salt makes the body retain water, which raises blood volume and can raise blood pressure, especially in people who are overweight or sensitive to sodium's effects. Limit sodium to less than 2,300 milligrams (about 1 teaspoon of table salt) a day (page 17). If you seem to be sodium sensitive, your doctor may suggest cutting back even further.

Don't smoke

Although smoking doesn't cause high blood pressure, it injures blood vessel walls, promoting the buildup of fatty deposits and clot formation.

Get the right minerals

Three key minerals—potassium, calcium, and magnesium—play a role in controlling blood pressure. Potassium balances sodium in the body, helping to prevent or control high blood pressure and reduce the risk of stroke. Potassium-rich foods include many fruits, vegetables, dairy foods, and fish.

Calcium has been shown to lower blood pressure. To get this benefit, consume 1,000 to 1,500 milligrams of calcium each day. Calcium-rich foods include low-fat or fat-free dairy products and green leafy vegetables. Magnesium also has a favorable effect on blood pressure. The best sources are whole grains, green leafy vegetables, nuts, seeds, and legumes.

Manage stress

Stress can briefly raise blood pressure and make hypertension harder to control. It can also boost harmful LDL cholesterol in the blood and heighten the blood's tendency to clot, raising heart attack and stroke risk. Ask your doctor for stress-control tips.

Take your medication

If your doctor has prescribed a blood pressure medication, always take it as prescribed—even if you feel fine. Uncontrolled high blood pressure can lead to heart attack, stroke, or kidney failure. If you notice side effects, call your doctor immediately. Do *not* stop taking the drug, a step that can cause your blood pressure to rise to a dangerously high level.

THE DASH DIET

An eating plan called Dietary Approaches to Stop Hypertension (or DASH) has been proven in studies to lower high blood pressure.

The DASH guidelines were used in developing the recipes in this book. They are low in total fat, saturated fat, and cholesterol and rich in fruits, vegetables, and low-fat dairy products. They also include whole grains, fish, poultry, and nuts and limit red meat, sweets, and sugary drinks. Many are rich in fiber, calcium, magnesium, and potassium.

The DASH diet was found to be most effective at lowering blood pressure when daily sodium intake is reduced from the recommended 2,300 milligrams a day to a daily intake of about 1,500 milligrams.

SETTING NUTRITION GOALS

A diet that can help you lower or better control your blood pressure and avoid the potential life-threatening complications of hypertension offers a wide range of nutritious and delicious food choices. You can achieve these health benefits by following some basic guidelines.

A hypertension-fighting diet limits calories and unhealthy saturated and trans fats. Eat mostly high-fiber plant foods such as whole grains, vegetables, and fruits and include plenty of low-fat or fat-free dairy products. Limit salt, added sugars, and red meat. Drink alcohol in moderation.

All foods are made up of carbohydrates, fats, and protein. Carbohydrates and fats are your body's main sources of fuel. Carbohydrates should make up 45 to 65 percent of your daily calories, fats (mostly from vegetable fats) 20 to 35 percent, and protein 12 to 20 percent.

HOW TO DISTRIBUTE YOUR DAILY CALORIES

45–65% 20–35% 12–20%

Carbohydrates Fats Protein

CARBOHYDRATES

Carbohydrates are the sugars, starches, and fiber that make up plant foods such as fruits, vegetables, and whole grains. For people who are at risk of hypertension and those who have it, whole grains and fiber are especially beneficial because they contain little sodium and they are rich in disease-fighting, artery-protecting antioxidants and phytochemicals.

Good carbs

Whole grains—the seeds of grasses such as wheat, oats, rice, corn, rye, barley, millet, kasha, and quinoa— are rich in heart-protecting B vitamins and the blood pressure– regulating minerals potassium, magnesium, and calcium (page 11).

Bad carbs

When stripped of their outer husk, grains lose most of their nutrients and fiber. These processed, refined foods—such as white bread, white rice, and white pasta—are digested faster than whole grains and provide little more than calories.

Fiber

Fiber is the indigestible part of plant foods. Soluble fiber—found mainly in whole grains such as oats, rye, and wheat—is especially beneficial for people who have high blood pressure or who want to avoid it. It improves cholesterol levels, reducing the risk of heart disease and stroke.

TEN A DAY?

Medical studies have shown that eating up to 10 servings of fruits and vegetables every day can reduce your risk of heart disease and stroke, two major complications of high blood pressure.

Eating ten servings a day sounds like a lot, but it's easier than you think. For example, you can get 3 servings of fruit at breakfast by having ½ cup of blueberries, a slice of melon, and ¾ cup of orange juice. Add a mid-morning snack of an apple, orange, or celery, or ½ cup of raisins or cut-up carrots, and you've reached 4 servings. Get 2 more servings at lunch with 2 cups of salad. Have a banana for dessert or for an afternoon snack, and you're up to 7 servings.

For dinner, try Hearty Minestrone Soup on page 37 or Roasted Root Vegetables on page 110. Each provides 2 servings of veggies; add ½ cup of cooked broccoli plus a salad and fruit for dessert and you're over 10 servings.

HEALTHY FATS

Fats from food provide energy, help the body absorb some vitamins, make food taste smooth, and make you feel full. Oils from vegetables, nuts, and seeds (called unsaturated fats) and fats from seafood (omega-3 fatty acids) help protect the heart and blood vessels and can lower blood pressure. Unsaturated fats are usually liquid at room temperature.

A healthy salad such as the one pictured, which includes iron-packed spinach and raspberries, is dressed with balsamic vinegar and olive oil, a monounsaturated fat.

Monounsaturated fats

These superhealthy fats come mainly from olive, canola, and peanut oils, most nuts, and avocados. They lower harmful LDL cholesterol in the blood, raise helpful HDL cholesterol, and cut triglycerides, easing the risk of heart disease and hypertension.

Polyunsaturated fats

Rich in omega-3 and omega-6 fatty acids, these lower LDL cholesterol, although they may also lower helpful HDL cholesterol. Good sources are corn, sunflower, safflower, flaxseed, and soybean oils and fatty fish such as salmon and albacore tuna.

Plant sterols

Found in nuts, soybeans, seeds, and many other plant foods, these substances slow the absorption of dietary cholesterol and can lower total cholesterol and harmful LDL cholesterol in the blood. Look for salad dressings with added plant sterols.

UNHEALTHY FATS

Some types of fats can harm your health, increasing your risk of heart disease, blood vessel problems, and stroke. The most damaging fats are saturated fats and trans fats, which are usually solid or semisolid at room temperature. These fats occur in many foods, so you need to make an extra effort to avoid them.

Saturated fats

Found in meat, dark-meat poultry and poultry skin, butter, full-fat dairy products, coconut oil, and palm oil, these fats raise total cholesterol and LDL cholesterol, boosting the risk of hypertension and heart disease. Limit them to less than 10 percent of your daily calories.

Trans fats

Vegetable oils can be hydrogenated, a process that extends shelf life and maintains the flavor of foods. But these "trans fats," found in margarines, shortening, and many processed and fast foods, raise total and harmful LDL cholesterol.

Dietary cholesterol

Found in foods of animal origin— including egg yolks, liver, shellfish, full-fat dairy products, and meat and poultry—dietary cholesterol can raise blood cholesterol, but not equally in everyone and not as significantly as do saturated fats and trans fats.

CUTTING BACK ON FAT

When figuring your daily intake of fat, consider the amount of fat you eat during the whole day, not just in one meal. If you indulge in a rich breakfast, limit the amount of fat in your lunch and dinner. Some tips:

• Make some meals meatless.

• Choose healthy fats such as olive and canola oils, avocados, and nuts.

• Avoid fatty meats, full-fat dairy products, rich baked goods, and anything with trans fats.

• Select foods that are fat free or low fat (3 grams of fat or less per serving). Products labeled "reduced fat" (25 percent less fat than in comparable foods) and "light" (50 percent less) are not low fat.

• Limit your dietary cholesterol to less than 300 mg a day, or 200 mg if you have heart disease.

PROTEIN

Protein, an essential nutrient found in both animal and plant foods, repairs tissues, builds muscle, and carries hormones and vitamins throughout the body via the bloodstream. Infants and children have the highest daily protein requirements pound for pound. Most American adults consume far more protein than they need (see box below).

HOW MUCH PROTEIN DO YOU NEED?

Adults need a surprisingly small amount of protein every day—only 0.365 grams per pound of body weight. This means that if you weigh 140 pounds, your daily requirement for protein is 51 grams (140 x 0.365 = 51).

It's easy to go over that amount. A 3-ounce chicken breast and a 2-cup bowl of black bean soup each provide nearly 30 grams of protein. In the chart below, use your weight to determine how much protein you may need in a day.

150 pounds – 55 grams

160 pounds – 59 grams

170 pounds – 62 grams

180 pounds – 66 grams

200 pounds – 73 grams

It's healthiest to get most of your protein from plant sources such as legumes and whole grains, along with low-fat dairy products and fish.

Animal proteins

Poultry, meat, milk, and eggs are rich in protein but can contain harmful fats and cholesterol (page 15). Look for lean meats and low-fat dairy products, remove the skin from poultry, and in recipes replace 1 egg with 2 egg whites. Fish is an excellent heart-healthy protein.

Plant proteins

Grains, beans and lentils, nuts, and some fruits and vegetables contain no cholesterol or unhealthy fats and are loaded with antioxidants and fiber. Vegetarians can get plenty of protein by combining whole grains, legumes, eggs, and dairy products.

High-protein diets

Low-carbohydrate, high-protein diets can result in rapid weight loss but may cause kidney problems in some people with hypertension; the long-term effects of these types of diets are unknown. Talk to your doctor before trying a high-protein diet.

SODIUM

Sodium in food is linked to high blood pressure. Although some people seem more sensitive to the effects of sodium than others, doctors advise everyone to limit their sodium intake to less than 2,300 milligrams a day.

Break the salt habit

Most of us eat several times as much sodium as we need. Much of the salt comes from processed, packaged, and fast foods—not from the salt shaker. An easy way to limit salt is to eat more fresh foods such as fruits, vegetables, and whole grains. Select foods with less than 140 milligrams of sodium per serving, or 5 percent of the daily recommendation.

REPLACE SALT WITH NEW FLAVORS

Reprogram your taste buds to savor flavors other than salt. Experiment with sodium-free flavorings such as herbs and spices; fresh lemon, lime, and orange juices; and garlic and onion powders. Add salt-free seasoning blends to soups, stews, and casseroles.

ALCOHOL

Moderate consumption of alcohol is linked to a reduced risk of heart disease, heart attack, and stroke. However, excess alcohol consumption can *increase* the risk of heart attack, high blood pressure, and stroke.

Drinking and blood pressure

It is not known precisely how alcohol affects blood pressure. But heavy drinking can damage the heart and blood vessels, boost blood pressure, and raise the risk of hypertension. Also, because alcohol interferes with the action of some blood pressure medications, heavy drinking can make hypertension harder to control.

WHAT'S MODERATE?

Moderate drinking is 1 drink a day for women and 2 drinks a day for men. A drink equals one 5-ounce glass of wine, a 12-ounce beer, or 1½ ounces of liquor. Despite the potential health benefits of moderate drinking, doctors do not recommend that people start drinking for their health.

KEEPING FAT UNDER CONTROL

Doctors recommend lowering the amount of harmful saturated and trans fats you eat to less than 10 percent of total daily calories or completely eliminating them from your diet. You should also limit total fat, including healthy fats (page 14), to less than 30 percent of daily calories. Follow the steps in the next few pages to estimate your daily fat allowance based on your calorie needs.

HOW TO FIND THE NUTRIENT VALUES IN EACH RECIPE

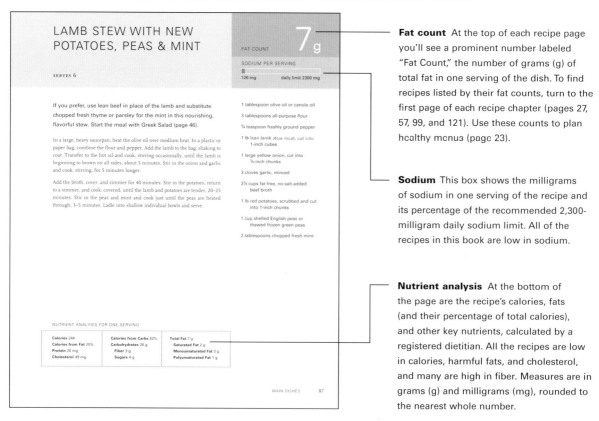

Fat count At the top of each recipe page you'll see a prominent number labeled "Fat Count," the number of grams (g) of total fat in one serving of the dish. To find recipes listed by their fat counts, turn to the first page of each recipe chapter (pages 27, 57, 99, and 121). Use these counts to plan healthy menus (page 23).

Sodium This box shows the milligrams of sodium in one serving of the recipe and its percentage of the recommended 2,300-milligram daily sodium limit. All of the recipes in this book are low in sodium.

Nutrient analysis At the bottom of the page are the recipe's calories, fats (and their percentage of total calories), and other key nutrients, calculated by a registered dietitian. All the recipes are low in calories, harmful fats, and cholesterol, and many are high in fiber. Measures are in grams (g) and milligrams (mg), rounded to the nearest whole number.

1 HOW ACTIVE ARE YOU?

Your activity level and weight determine the amount of food you should eat. The more frequent and intense your physical activity, the more food energy—calories—you burn. If you want to lose weight, you'll need to raise your level of activity *and* reduce the amount of food you eat. Read the descriptions below to find the activity level that best describes yours.

Take your activity level and go to step 2 →

INACTIVE

Mainly sedentary most days of the week. Daily activities limited to driving, reading, watching TV, using the computer, and cooking with only rare, light exertion such as shopping.

SOMEWHAT ACTIVE

Moderate activity throughout the week. Activities include light housework, leisurely walks, playing with children, climbing stairs, and low-intensity sports such as golf or bowling.

ACTIVE

Vigorous exercise several days a week. Activities include brisk walks, jogging, gardening, long bike rides, gym workouts, tennis or racquetball, swimming, dancing, or yoga.

THE BENEFITS OF EXERCISE

If exercise could be packed into a pill, it would be the single most-prescribed medication because of the many health benefits it confers.

Exercise promotes weight loss, improves cholesterol levels, and lowers blood pressure, all of which reduce your risk of heart disease and stroke.

Exercise also reduces the risk of type 2 diabetes, the bone-thinning disorder osteoporosis, and even some types of cancer.

Physical activity is good for the brain, as well. It increases blood flow, improves sleep, lifts mood and energy level, and heightens alertness and memory.

Continuing to exercise as you age may even reduce your risk of Alzheimer's disease and other forms of dementia.

Exercise to lower blood pressure

Even a moderate amount of exercise—just 30 minutes of brisk walking three times a week—can lower your blood pressure by up to 10 points. Regular exercise can also help you lose weight and maintain a healthy weight. A modest 5- or 10-pound weight loss can lower blood pressure, and if you have moderate hypertension, it may be enough to bring your blood pressure down to normal.

2 FIND YOUR CALORIE NEEDS

To determine how many calories you can eat each day to stay at your current weight, find your weight on the far left side of the chart below and locate your daily calorie allowance to the right in the column that corresponds to your activity level. To lose a pound a week, subtract 500 calories from that daily total.

> Take your calorie needs and go to step 3 →

LOSE WEIGHT SENSIBLY

The only sure way to lose weight is to burn more calories than you consume—that is, exercise more and eat less. A sensible approach is to lose 1 or 2 pounds a week. With that plan, you're more likely to keep the weight off over the long term, giving you better control over your blood pressure.

Plan more meals and snacks around whole grains, vegetables, and fruits. And cut back on calories by watching portion sizes and lightening up on high-fat and sugary treats and fast foods. Here are some examples.

• To save 80 calories, have an apple instead of 4 shortbread cookies.

• To save 110 calories, eat ½ cup of low-fat frozen yogurt instead of a 1½-ounce chocolate bar.

• To save more than 200 calories, order a 3-ounce hamburger instead of a 6-ounce one.

WEIGHT (in pounds)	INACTIVE	SOMEWHAT ACTIVE	ACTIVE
120	1500	1700	1800
130	1600	1800	1900
140	1700	1900	2100
150	1800	2000	2200
160	2000	2100	2400
170	2100	2300	2500
180	2200	2400	2700
190	2300	2500	2800
200	2500	2700	3000
210	2600	2800	3100
220	2700	3000	3300
230	2800	3100	3400
240	2900	3200	3600
250	3100	3300	3700
260	3200	3500	3900
270	3300	3600	4000
280	3400	3700	4100

CALORIES

3 LOCATE YOUR FAT COUNT

For most people, doctors say, fats should make up 30 percent or less
of the total calories they eat in a day. Depending on your health risks,
your doctor may recommend a lower daily fat limit (see "What's Your Fat
Percentage?," right). In this chart, locate the box with your daily calorie
allowance to find the number of grams (g) of fat you should eat in a day.

CALORIES	FAT	CALORIES	FAT	CALORIES	FAT
1500	50g	2400	80g	3300	110g
1600	53g	2500	83g	3400	113g
1700	57g	2600	87g	3500	117g
1800	60g	2700	90g	3600	120g
1900	63g	2800	93g	3700	123g
2000	67g	2900	97g	3800	127g
2100	70g	3000	100g	3900	130g
2200	73g	3100	103g	4000	133g
2300	77g	3200	107g	4100	137g

WHAT'S YOUR FAT PERCENTAGE?

The chart at left shows the number
of fat grams that equal 30 percent
of total daily calories. If your doctor
has recommended eating less fat,
use the following easy formula to
calculate your daily fat allotment.

Let's say your daily calorie need is
1800 and your recommended daily
fat is 25 percent of total calories.

1 Multiply your daily calories (1800)
by 25 percent (0.25).
1800 x 0.25 = 450
This means 450 of your daily
calories can come from fat.

2 Divide your daily fat calories (450)
by nine, which is the number of
calories in 1 gram of fat.
450 ÷ 9 = 50
Your daily fat count is 50 grams.

Keep notes on the fat grams you
consume each day. Check the per-
serving fat grams on food labels and
the per-serving nutrient analyses of
recipes, including those in this book.

COOKING FOR THE FAMILY

You can help your children avoid high blood pressure and other health problems by getting them in the habit of making smart food choices. Be a good role model and cook and eat as many meals together as you can.

Make time for breakfast

Eating breakfast jump-starts your metabolism and helps you burn more calories throughout the day. It's especially important for children, because it promotes proper growth and improves school performance. Healthy breakfasts include a bowl of unsweetened cereal with skim milk and a piece of fruit; a container of low-fat yogurt mixed with sliced fruit and crunchy cereal; or hot oatmeal with dried fruit, low-fat vanilla yogurt, and a glass of skim milk.

Kid-friendly lunches

Encourage your kids to look beyond peanut butter and jelly sandwiches. If they get lunch at school, make sure the meals served are low in fat, calories, and added sugars. If not, suggest that the school offer some healthier choices and eliminate high-calorie foods such as pizza, fries, soft drinks, and candy bars. At home, try making sandwiches with whole-grain breads, lean meats and poultry, low-fat mayonnaise or mustard, and lettuce, tomato, and other vegetables.

CHOOSE FATS WISELY

Because saturated and trans fats are most harmful to blood cholesterol, you should limit them to less than 8 to 10 percent of your daily calories, or less than a third of your fat each day. Here's how to cut back.

• Shop for low-fat or fat-free milk, yogurt, and frozen desserts.

• Buy packaged foods made without hydrogenated vegetable oils, palm oil, or coconut oil. Avoid deep-fried foods such as french fries.

• Cook with vegetable oils instead of butter or margarine.

• Remove skin from poultry and trim fat from meats before cooking.

• Buy prepared foods that contain less than 1 gram of saturated fat per serving.

Tips for cutting calories

Eat only when you're hungry.

Eat slowly (it takes 20 to 30 minutes to start feeling full), and stop eating when you're full.

Begin meals with a large glass of water.

Have a fruit or vegetable for a snack; have fruit for dessert.

Choose skinless poultry and lean cuts of meat.

Choose low-fat or fat-free cheeses, salad dressings, and bread spreads.

Use low-fat cooking methods such as baking, broiling, grilling, or steaming; choose cooking sprays for stir-fries and sautéing.

Keep a food log to help you track how much you're eating.

PLANNING HEALTHY MEALS

Preparing healthy meals does not need to be time consuming or difficult. As an example, we have listed a sample day's menu of dishes from this book for nutritious, satisfying meals that you and your family will enjoy. Furthermore, because the recipes in this book are so low in sodium, they are perfect choices for a blood pressure–friendly diet.

These generous menus showcase how easy it can be to eat well and still maintain a diet that falls within the recommended daily sodium limit of 2,300 milligrams. Be sure to also keep track of your daily fat and calorie intake.

Breakfast (per serving)	212 mg
Tropical Fruit Salad (page 127)	22 mg
1 cup low-fat yogurt	190 mg

Lunch (per serving)	643 mg
Lemon-Rice Soup (page 43)	473 mg
Greek Salad (page 46)	170 mg

Snack (per serving)	119 mg
Buttermilk Corn Muffin (page 119)	119 mg

Dinner (per serving)	453 g
Dijon-Orange Pork Chops (page 81)	395 mg
Thyme-Scented Mushrooms (page 112)	54 mg
Pear Crumble (page 125)	4 mg

Day's total sodium	1,427 mg

HEALTHY SNACKS TO KEEP ON HAND

ORANGES
Peeled and pulled apart into segments or cut into wedges, oranges are vitamin C–packed breakfast favorites that help your body absorb iron.

GRAPES
A perfect low-calorie treat, grapes are 80 percent water, with only 60 calories in a cup. Kids love them because they're sweet, juicy, and fun to eat.

BERRIES
These colorful, nutrient-dense fruits make great toppings for cereal and yogurt, add richness to smoothies, and freeze well and thaw quickly for a refreshing snack.

BANANAS
Bananas are neatly packaged by nature and easy to slip into a lunch box or sack. Available year round, they are rich in healthy carbohydrates and potassium.

KIWIFRUIT
Kiwifruit comes in its own serving cup: Just cut it in half and scoop out the flesh with a spoon. Or, for a nicer presentation, peel the skin and cut the flesh into slices.

DRIED FRUIT
When dried, fruits lose moisture and gain a longer shelf life. But dried fruits are much higher in calories and sugar than fresh ones, so watch portion sizes.

CARROTS

Rich in vitamin A and beta carotene, carrots are favorites of both children and adults. Eat them whole, cut into sticks, or shredded in salads.

NONFAT YOGURT

Plain yogurt is an excellent source of bone-building calcium and one of the healthiest foods you can eat. Mix it with fruit for sundaes or smoothies.

TOMATOES

Cherished in many cuisines, tomatoes are known cancer fighters. Keep the cherry and grape varieties out in a bowl for snacking.

POPCORN

Air-popped popcorn is sugar free, fat free, low in calories, and high in fiber, making it an especially smart family treat. Add to dried fruit and nuts for a trail mix.

UNSALTED NUTS

Eating a handful of nuts a day is good for your heart. What's more, because nuts are so satisfying, they may even help you lose weight. Keep a variety on hand.

STRING CHEESE

Kids love string cheese—the pull-apart food—which makes it an easy way to supply them with calcium for their growing bones and teeth.

STARTERS, SOUPS & SALADS

BELL PEPPER SLICES WITH
BLACK BEAN DIP, 28

ROASTED ASPARAGUS & LEEKS, 32

COLESLAW WITH
APPLE & HORSERADISH, 48

SUN-DRIED TOMATO TOASTS, 31

SPICY ROASTED RED PEPPER
SPREAD, 34

BUTTERNUT SQUASH SOUP, 38

GREEK SALAD, 46

TOMATO-BASIL SALAD WITH
FETA CHEESE, 50

FRESH CORN SALAD, 45

HEARTY MINESTRONE SOUP, 37

WHITE BEAN, SAUSAGE
& KALE SOUP, 42

LEMON-RICE SOUP, 43

THREE-BEAN SALAD, 49

SPINACH SALAD WITH FRUIT
& BLUE CHEESE, 53

TOMATO SOUP WITH PASTA
& CHICKPEAS, 41

CRAB, ARUGULA & AVOCADO
SALAD, 54

1 g

BELL PEPPER SLICES WITH BLACK BEAN DIP

SERVES 4

3 bell peppers, preferably a combination of red and yellow

One 15-oz can no-salt-added black beans, drained but not rinsed

1 small tomato, seeded (page 67) and chopped

¼ cup chopped green onion or fresh cilantro

2 teaspoons seeded and minced jalapeño chile

½ teaspoon chili powder

½ teaspoon ground cumin

1 clove garlic, minced

Bell peppers cut into curved "scoops" are perfect for dipping. Not rinsing the beans keeps the dip moist and the preparation time short. You can substitute 2 cups cooked dried black beans for the canned beans.

Cut the bell peppers in half lengthwise and remove the stems, seeds, and ribs. Cut each half lengthwise into four pieces. Set aside.

Place the beans in a bowl. Using a potato masher or wooden spoon, partially mash the beans. Add the tomato, green onion, jalapeño, chili powder, cumin, and garlic and stir to mix well. Serve at room temperature with the bell pepper pieces for dipping.

NUTRIENT ANALYSIS FOR ONE SERVING

Calories 125	**Calories from Carbs** 74%	**Total Fat** 1 g
Calories from Fat 4%	**Carbohydrates** 24 g	**Saturated Fat** 0 g
Protein 7 g	**Fiber** 8 g	**Monounsaturated Fat** 0 g
Cholesterol 0 mg	**Sugars** 6 g	**Polyunsaturated Fat** 0 g

SUN-DRIED TOMATO TOASTS

SERVES 4

Toast the baguette slices under a preheated broiler or in batches in a toaster oven. If preferred, substitute crisp whole-grain crackers for the toasts. Serve as a first course to Braised Chicken with Dried Plums & Almonds (page 75).

In a bowl, combine the tomato, sun-dried tomatoes, basil, garlic, and red pepper flakes and toss gently to mix well. Spoon the tomato mixture onto the toasts just before serving.

1 large tomato, seeded (page 67) and chopped

¼ cup chopped, drained, oil-packed sun-dried tomatoes

2 tablespoons chopped fresh basil or parsley

1 clove garlic, minced

⅛ teaspoon red pepper flakes or freshly ground black pepper

16 slices whole-wheat baguette, ½ inch thick, toasted

NUTRIENT ANALYSIS FOR ONE SERVING

Calories 94	**Calories from Carbs** 68%	**Total Fat** 2 g
Calories from Fat 18%	**Carbohydrates** 18 g	**Saturated Fat** 0 g
Protein 4 g	**Fiber** 3 g	**Monounsaturated Fat** 1 g
Cholesterol 0 mg	**Sugars** 3 g	**Polyunsaturated Fat** 0 g

1 g

ROASTED ASPARAGUS & LEEKS

SERVES 4

1 bunch of asparagus spears, trimmed and cut into 1-inch pieces (about 3 cups)

1 large or 2 small leeks, including tender green parts, thinly sliced (about 1 cup)

2 tablespoons fat-free, no-salt-added vegetable broth

1 teaspoon olive oil

¼ teaspoon freshly ground pepper

2 teaspoons balsamic vinegar

Serve this light but smoky-flavored dish as a starter or as a side dish for Fettuccini with Fresh Tomato Sauce (page 93). Rinse the leeks thoroughly to remove sand and dirt. Vidalia, Walla Walla, Maui, or other sweet onions may be used in place of the leeks.

Preheat the oven to 400°F.

In a large jelly-roll pan or roasting pan, toss together the asparagus, leek, broth, olive oil, and pepper until evenly coated. Arrange in a single layer in the pan and roast until the asparagus is tender, 12–15 minutes. Drizzle the vinegar over the vegetables and toss well. Transfer to a platter or individual plates and serve immediately.

NUTRIENT ANALYSIS FOR ONE SERVING

Calories 48	**Calories from Carbs** 59%	**Total Fat** 1 g
Calories from Fat 23%	**Carbohydrates** 8 g	**Saturated Fat** 0 g
Protein 2 g	**Fiber** 2 g	**Monounsaturated Fat** 1 g
Cholesterol 0 mg	**Sugars** 3 g	**Polyunsaturated Fat** 0 g

SODIUM PER SERVING

180 mg   daily limit 2300 mg

SPICY ROASTED RED PEPPER SPREAD

SERVES 4

¼ lb reduced-fat silken tofu

⅓ cup jarred roasted red bell peppers, drained

10 pitted Kalamata olives

1 teaspoon extra-virgin olive oil

½ teaspoon ground cumin

⅛ teaspoon cayenne pepper

8 large whole-wheat crackers

Try this tangy, easy-to-make spread on a variety of whole-grain crackers. If large crackers aren't available, use 16 smaller ones. Top the crackers with a swirl of red pepper spread as a colorful starter for Chicken Provençal (page 74).

In a food processor or blender, combine the tofu, roasted red peppers, olives, olive oil, cumin, and cayenne. Process to a purée, scraping down the sides of the work bowl once. Transfer to a serving bowl. Serve immediately with the crackers, or cover and refrigerate for up to 24 hours.

NUTRIENT ANALYSIS FOR ONE SERVING

Calories 71	**Calories from Carbs** 56%	**Total Fat** 2 g
Calories from Fat 26%	**Carbohydrates** 10 g	**Saturated Fat** 0 g
Protein 3 g	**Fiber** 1 g	**Monounsaturated Fat** 1 g
Cholesterol 0 mg	**Sugars** 1 g	**Polyunsaturated Fat** 0 g

HEARTY MINESTRONE SOUP

SERVES 5

Following the Italian tradition, this satisfying minestrone soup contains vegetables, beans, and cheese. For even more visual appeal, use half zucchini and half yellow squash. Serve as a starter or as a main course.

In a saucepan, heat the olive oil over medium heat. Add the garlic and sauté for 1 minute. Add the broth, squash, basil, oregano, and red pepper flakes and bring to a simmer. Simmer, uncovered, for 5 minutes. Stir in the tomatoes and beans. Return to a simmer and cook, stirring occasionally, until the tomatoes and beans are heated through, about 5 minutes longer.

Ladle the soup into individual bowls, sprinkle with the cheese, and serve immediately.

2 teaspoons olive oil

3 cloves garlic, minced

3 cups fat-free, no-salt-added vegetable or chicken broth

1 zucchini or yellow crookneck squash, diced

1 tablespoon chopped fresh basil or 1 teaspoon dried basil

1 tablespoon chopped fresh oregano or 1 teaspoon dried oregano

⅛ teaspoon red pepper flakes or freshly ground black pepper

3 plum tomatoes, cored and diced, or 1 cup drained canned no-salt-added tomatoes, diced

One 15-oz can no-salt-added red beans or red kidney beans, rinsed and drained

⅓ cup grated Romano or Parmesan cheese

NUTRIENT ANALYSIS FOR ONE SERVING

Calories 136	**Calories from Carbs** 54%	**Total Fat** 4 g
Calories from Fat 25%	**Carbohydrates** 19 g	**Saturated Fat** 1 g
Protein 7 g	**Fiber** 6 g	**Monounsaturated Fat** 2 g
Cholesterol 7 mg	**Sugars** 2 g	**Polyunsaturated Fat** 2 g

BUTTERNUT SQUASH SOUP

SERVES 4

1 small butternut squash, about
   2 lb (see note)

1¾ cups fat-free, no-salt-added
   vegetable or chicken broth

¾ cup unsweetened apple juice

¼ teaspoon freshly grated nutmeg

1 tablespoon unsalted butter

1 leek, including tender green
   parts, thinly sliced (about ¾ cup)

½ cup fat-free croutons (optional)

This warming and beautifully colored soup is a cheering dish in winter. Two 12-oz packages of frozen puréed butternut squash can be substituted for fresh squash to save time. Thinly sliced sweet onion, such as Vidalia, may be substituted for the leek.

In a saucepan fitted with a steamer basket, bring 1 inch of water to a boil. Cut the squash in half lengthwise and, using a spoon, scoop out the seeds and any fibers. Using a sharp vegetable peeler or a small, sharp knife, peel away the skin. Cut the squash into 1-inch cubes and place in the steamer basket. Steam until tender, 10–12 minutes. Transfer to a bowl or the work bowl of a food processor. Using a potato masher or with the food processor, mash or process the squash to a smooth purée.

In a saucepan over high heat, combine the squash, broth, apple juice, and nutmeg. Bring to a boil, stirring occasionally. Reduce the heat to medium-low and simmer, uncovered, for 10 minutes, stirring occasionally, to allow the flavors to blend.

Meanwhile, in a small frying pan over medium heat, melt the butter. Add the leek and cook, stirring frequently, until golden brown and crisp, 7–8 minutes.

Ladle the soup into individual bowls, top with the fried leeks and the croutons, if using, and serve immediately.

NUTRIENT ANALYSIS FOR ONE SERVING

Calories 155	**Calories from Carbs** 78%	**Total Fat** 2 g
Calories from Fat 14%	**Carbohydrates** 31 g	**Saturated Fat** 2 g
Protein 3 g	**Fiber** 2 g	**Monounsaturated Fat** 0 g
Cholesterol 6 mg	**Sugars** 9 g	**Polyunsaturated Fat** 0 g

TOMATO SOUP WITH PASTA & CHICKPEAS

SERVES 4

The inclusion of beans and pasta gives tomato soup plenty of protein and fiber, in addition to extra flavor. You can substitute 2 cups cooked dried chickpeas for the canned beans.

In a saucepan, heat the olive oil over medium-high heat. Add the garlic and sauté for 1 minute. Add the broth and pasta and bring to a boil. Reduce the heat to medium-low and simmer, uncovered, for 5 minutes. Stir in the tomatoes, chickpeas, and red pepper flakes. Return to a simmer and cook, stirring occasionally, until the pasta is tender, about 5 minutes longer. Remove from the heat and stir in the oregano.

Ladle the soup into individual bowls, sprinkle with the Parmesan, and serve immediately.

2 teaspoons olive oil

2 cloves garlic, minced

1¾ cups fat-free, no-salt-added vegetable or chicken broth

½ cup dried whole-wheat elbow macaroni or gemelli pasta

One 14½-oz can no-salt-added whole tomatoes, with juice, coarsely chopped

One 15-oz can no-salt-added chickpeas (garbanzo beans), rinsed and drained

⅛ teaspoon red pepper flakes or cayenne pepper

1 tablespoon chopped fresh oregano, marjoram, or basil or 1 teaspoon dried

¼ cup grated Parmesan cheese

NUTRIENT ANALYSIS FOR ONE SERVING

Calories 217	**Calories from Carbs** 54%	**Total Fat** 6 g
Calories from Fat 25%	**Carbohydrates** 29 g	**Saturated Fat** 2 g
Protein 11 g	**Fiber** 7 g	**Monounsaturated Fat** 2 g
Cholesterol 8 mg	**Sugars** 4 g	**Polyunsaturated Fat** 0 g

4g

WHITE BEAN, SAUSAGE & KALE SOUP

SERVES 5

2 teaspoons olive oil

3 cloves garlic, minced

3½ cups fat-free, no-salt-added chicken broth

½ lb kale or Swiss chard, thick ribs and stems cut away, leaves coarsely chopped (about 3 cups)

2 links fully cooked spicy chicken sausage, about 4½ oz, chopped

One 15-oz can no-salt-added navy or Great Northern beans, rinsed and drained

2 tablespoons chopped fresh basil

If you like, substitute 3 cups baby spinach leaves for the kale and stir it in during the last minute of cooking. You can use 2 cups cooked dried white beans for the canned beans.

In a saucepan, heat the olive oil over high heat. Add the garlic and sauté for 30 seconds. Add the broth and kale and bring to a boil. Stir in the sausage, reduce the heat to medium-low, and simmer, uncovered, for 10 minutes, to allow the flavors to blend. Stir in the beans, return to a simmer, and cook until the beans are heated through, about 1 minute longer. Remove from the heat and stir in the basil. Ladle into individual bowls and serve.

NUTRIENT ANALYSIS FOR ONE SERVING

Calories 170	**Calories from Carbs** 43%	**Total Fat** 4 g
Calories from Fat 22%	**Carbohydrates** 19 g	**Saturated Fat** 1 g
Protein 15 g	**Fiber** 6 g	**Monounsaturated Fat** 2 g
Cholesterol 14 mg	**Sugars** 0 g	**Polyunsaturated Fat** 0 g

LEMON-RICE SOUP

FAT COUNT

4g

SODIUM PER SERVING

473 mg   daily limit 2300 mg

SERVES 4

Based on the classic Greek egg and lemon soup *avgolemono,* this version comes together quickly and is both light and satisfying. To save time, substitute quick-cooking brown rice, which cooks in about 10 minutes, for regular brown rice.

In a saucepan over high heat, combine the broth and rice and bring to a boil. Reduce the heat to low and simmer gently until the rice is tender, about 45 minutes.

When the rice is done, in a bowl, beat together the eggs and lemon juice. To prevent the eggs from curdling, gradually add about ½ cup of the hot broth to the egg mixture while stirring constantly. Gradually add the mixture to the soup, again stirring constantly. Ladle the soup into individual shallow bowls, sprinkle with the Parmesan, and serve immediately.

4 cups fat-free, no-salt-added chicken broth

¾ cup long-grain brown rice

2 large eggs

2 tablespoons fresh lemon juice

2 tablespoons grated Parmesan or Romano cheese

NUTRIENT ANALYSIS FOR ONE SERVING

Calories 168	**Calories from Carbs** 51%	**Total Fat** 4 g
Calories from Fat 22%	**Carbohydrates** 21 g	**Saturated Fat** 1 g
Protein 11 g	**Fiber** 1 g	**Monounsaturated Fat** 1 g
Cholesterol 108 mg	**Sugars** 1 g	**Polyunsaturated Fat** 1 g

FRESH CORN SALAD

SERVES 4

Take advantage of the abundance of corn in the summer months with this refreshing salad. The corn kernels are cut right off the cob, keeping their sweetness and juiciness. If fresh corn is not available, use 2 cups thawed frozen corn kernels.

Hold an ear of corn upright in a bowl, stem end down. Using a sharp knife, cut down the length of the ear, cutting as close to the cob as possible, allowing the kernels to fall into the bowl and rotating the cob after each cut. Run the back of the knife blade along the length of the corn to squeeze out all the juice. Repeat with the remaining 3 ears.

In a large bowl, combine the corn kernels and their juice, pimientos, jalapeño, olive oil, lime juice, and pepper and toss to mix. Cover and refrigerate for at least 30 minutes or up to 24 hours.

Line each individual plate with a lettuce leaf. Divide the salad among the lettuce-lined plates and serve.

- 4 ears of fresh corn, husks and silk removed
- 1 2-oz jar sliced pimientos, drained, or ⅓ cup jarred roasted red bell peppers, drained and chopped
- 1½ teaspoons seeded and minced jalapeño chile
- 2 teaspoons olive oil
- 2 teaspoons fresh lime or lemon juice
- ⅛ teaspoon freshly ground pepper
- 4 large red leaf or butter (Boston) lettuce leaves

NUTRIENT ANALYSIS FOR ONE SERVING

Calories 103	**Calories from Carbs** 67%	**Total Fat** 3 g
Calories from Fat 23%	**Carbohydrates** 19 g	**Saturated Fat** 0 g
Protein 3 g	**Fiber** 3 g	**Monounsaturated Fat** 2 g
Cholesterol 0 mg	**Sugars** 1 g	**Polyunsaturated Fat** 1 g

GREEK SALAD

SERVES 4

2 tablespoons red wine vinegar

1½ teaspoons honey

8 large romaine (cos) lettuce
   leaves, sliced

1 cup sliced unpeeled English
(hothouse) or pickling cucumber

4 plum tomatoes, cored and
   quartered lengthwise

¼ cup sliced pitted Niçoise or
   Kalamata olives

¼ cup crumbled reduced-fat feta
   cheese

¼ teaspoon freshly ground pepper

This classic Mediterranean salad gets richness from feta cheese and olives but fits easily into a heart-healthy diet. Because unpeeled cucumbers are preferred for this dish, avoid using cucumbers that have wax on the skins.

In a small bowl, whisk together the vinegar and honey. Set aside.

Divide the lettuce among individual plates. Arrange the cucumber slices, tomato quarters, olives, and feta on each lettuce-lined plate. Drizzle the vinaigrette over the salads. Season with the pepper and serve.

NUTRIENT ANALYSIS FOR ONE SERVING

Calories 52	**Calories from Carbs** 50%	**Total Fat** 2 g
Calories from Fat 31%	**Carbohydrates** 7 g	**Saturated Fat** 1 g
Protein 3 g	**Fiber** 2 g	**Monounsaturated Fat** 1 g
Cholesterol 3 mg	**Sugars** 5 g	**Polyunsaturated Fat** 0 g

COLESLAW WITH APPLE & HORSERADISH

SERVES 4

½ head red cabbage, trimmed, cored, and thinly sliced or shredded (about 4 cups)

1 apple such as Gala or Fuji, unpeeled, cored and finely chopped or shredded

½ cup low-fat plain yogurt

2 tablespoons prepared horseradish

2 teaspoons honey (optional)

This colorful coleslaw improves in flavor as it chills. Because the apple is not peeled, be sure to scrub it under warm water to remove any waxy residue. Don't be wary of the horseradish; its earthy kick perfectly complements the flavor of the cabbage.

In a large bowl, combine the cabbage, apple, yogurt, horseradish, and honey, if using; toss well. Cover and refrigerate for at least 30 minutes or up to 24 hours before serving.

NUTRIENT ANALYSIS FOR ONE SERVING

Calories 59	**Calories from Carbs** 74%	**Total Fat** 1 g
Calories from Fat 8%	**Carbohydrates** 12 g	**Saturated Fat** 0 g
Protein 3 g	**Fiber** 2 g	**Monounsaturated Fat** 0 g
Cholesterol 2 mg	**Sugars** 10 g	**Polyunsaturated Fat** 0 g

THREE-BEAN SALAD

SERVES 6

This hearty, colorful summer favorite is a good source of fiber and protein. Adapt it for winter menus by substituting thawed frozen green and yellow wax beans. Small, reddish-brown adzuki beans are sweet, but other red beans also work well.

Bring a saucepan three-fourths full of water to a boil. Add the green and yellow beans and blanch for 1 minute. Drain the beans and immerse in cold water for 5 minutes to stop the cooking. Drain again and set aside.

In a large bowl, whisk together the olive oil, vinegar, mustard, tarragon, and pepper. Add the red, green, and yellow beans and the onion; toss well. Cover and refrigerate for at least 30 minutes or for up to 24 hours before serving.

To serve, line each individual plate with a lettuce leaf. Divide the salad among the lettuce-lined plates and serve.

3 oz green beans, trimmed and cut into 1-inch pieces

3 oz yellow wax beans, trimmed and cut into 1-inch pieces

1½ tablespoons olive oil

1½ tablespoons balsamic vinegar

1½ tablespoons Dijon mustard

1 tablespoon chopped fresh tarragon or 1 teaspoon dried tarragon

½ teaspoon freshly ground pepper

One 15-oz can no-salt-added adzuki beans, red beans, or red kidney beans, rinsed and drained

¼ cup finely diced red onion

6 large butter (Boston) or red leaf lettuce leaves

NUTRIENT ANALYSIS FOR ONE SERVING

Calories 136	**Calories from Carbs** 56%	**Total Fat** 5 g
Calories from Fat 26%	**Carbohydrates** 20 g	**Saturated Fat** 1 g
Protein 6 g	**Fiber** 6 g	**Monounsaturated Fat** 3 g
Cholesterol 0 mg	**Sugars** 1 g	**Polyunsaturated Fat** 1 g

TOMATO-BASIL SALAD WITH FETA CHEESE

SERVES 4

4 large ripe tomatoes (see note)

4 large butter (Boston) or romaine (cos) lettuce leaves

½ cup crumbled reduced-fat feta cheese

2 tablespoons chopped fresh basil or parsley

2 tablespoons balsamic vinegar

¼ teaspoon freshly ground pepper

This simple salad is best prepared with vine-ripened tomatoes. In the summer, look for colorful heirloom tomatoes at farmers' markets. In the winter, use a mixture of hothouse varieties and cherry or yellow teardrop tomatoes.

Slice larger tomatoes and cut smaller ones in half.

Line each individual plate with a lettuce leaf. Divide the tomatoes, feta, and basil among the lettuce-lined plates. Drizzle the vinegar over the salads, season with the pepper, and serve.

NUTRIENT ANALYSIS FOR ONE SERVING

Calories 67	**Calories from Carbs** 50%	**Total Fat** 2 g
Calories from Fat 24%	**Carbohydrates** 9 g	**Saturated Fat** 1 g
Protein 5 g	**Fiber** 2 g	**Monounsaturated Fat** .5 g
Cholesterol 5 mg	**Sugars** 6 g	**Polyunsaturated Fat** .5 g

SPINACH SALAD WITH FRUIT & BLUE CHEESE

FAT COUNT 4g

SODIUM PER SERVING

170 mg   daily limit 2300 mg

SERVES 4

Vitamin-packed fresh spinach is complemented by sweet fruit and tangy cheese. Try other combinations, such as sliced strawberries in place of the raspberries and goat cheese instead of blue cheese. Freeze goat cheese briefly for easier crumbling.

In a large bowl, combine the spinach, pear, raspberries, and blue cheese. In a small bowl, whisk together the vinegar, olive oil, mustard, and pepper. Drizzle the vinaigrette over the salad. Toss gently until the ingredients are evenly distributed. Transfer to individual plates and serve.

6 cups firmly packed baby spinach or torn spinach leaves

1 ripe but firm red Bartlett (Williams) or Comice pear, unpeeled, cored, and diced

1 cup fresh raspberries

2 tablespoons crumbled blue cheese

1 tablespoon balsamic vinegar

2 teaspoons extra-virgin olive oil

1 teaspoon Dijon mustard

⅛ teaspoon freshly ground pepper

NUTRIENT ANALYSIS FOR ONE SERVING

Calories 97	**Calories from Carbs** 62%	**Total Fat** 4 g
Calories from Fat 30%	**Carbohydrates** 17 g	**Saturated Fat** 1 g
Protein 2 g	**Fiber** 5 g	**Monounsaturated Fat** 2 g
Cholesterol 3 mg	**Sugars** 6 g	**Polyunsaturated Fat** 0 g

8 g

CRAB, ARUGULA & AVOCADO SALAD

SERVES 4

2 tablespoons fresh orange juice

1 tablespoon fresh lime juice

1 teaspoon honey

4 cups firmly packed arugula (rocket) leaves

4 oz fresh lump crabmeat, picked over for shell fragments and flaked

½ ripe avocado, pitted, peeled, and thinly sliced

½ teaspoon finely shredded or grated orange zest (page 139)

If arugula is unavailable, substitute mesclun salad mix or baby spring greens. You can also use all-white canned lump crabmeat, well drained, in place of the fresh crabmeat. Work quickly after peeling the avocado; it will discolor as it sits.

In a small bowl, whisk together the orange juice, lime juice, and honey.

Divide the arugula among individual plates. Arrange the crabmeat and avocado slices on each serving. Drizzle the salads with the citrus dressing, sprinkle with the orange zest, and serve immediately.

NUTRIENT ANALYSIS FOR ONE SERVING

Calories 119	**Calories from Carbs** 44%	**Total Fat** 8 g
Calories from Fat 31%	**Carbohydrates** 14 g	**Saturated Fat** 1 g
Protein 8 g	**Fiber** 2 g	**Monounsaturated Fat** 2 g
Cholesterol 20 mg	**Sugars** 3 g	**Polyunsaturated Fat** 1 g

MAIN DISHES

MEDITERRANEAN HALIBUT, 67

LEMON-GARLIC CHICKEN
SKEWERS, 68

PAN-SEARED SCALLOPS WITH
GARLIC & BASIL, 64

BAKED RED SNAPPER WITH
MEXICAN SPICES, 66

DIJON-ORANGE PORK CHOPS, 81

SPICY BROILED CATFISH, 58

ROASTED DUCK BREASTS WITH
RED WINE SAUCE, 73

VEAL SCALOPPINE, 85

SPANISH OMELET, 96

CHICKEN PROVENÇAL, 74

PORK CUTLETS WITH CUMIN
& LIME, 84

PORK TENDERLOIN WITH APPLE-
SAGE STUFFING, 82

SPAGHETTI WITH TOMATOES
& SHRIMP, 88

CHINESE CHICKEN SALAD, 70

BRAISED CHICKEN WITH DRIED
PLUMS & ALMONDS, 75

LAMB STEW WITH NEW POTATOES,
PEAS & MINT, 87

FETTUCCINE WITH FRESH TOMATO
SAUCE, 93

GRILLED LEMON TROUT, 62

WHITE BEAN CASSEROLE, 92

SOY-GLAZED SALMON WITH GARLIC
SPINACH, 61

GARLIC STEAK & POLENTA, 78

GRILLED PORTOBELLO
SANDWICHES, 91

BELL PEPPERS STUFFED WITH
BEANS & RICE, 95

BEEF & VEGETABLE FAJITAS, 76

Pan-Seared Scallops with Garlic & Basil, 64

SODIUM PER SERVING

97 mg   daily limit 2300 mg

SPICY BROILED CATFISH

SERVES 4

2 tablespoons yellow cornmeal

1 teaspoon paprika

½ teaspoon dried thyme

¼ teaspoon cayenne pepper

¼ teaspoon freshly ground black
  pepper

4 skinless catfish fillets, about 4 oz
  each

1½ teaspoons canola oil or olive oil

4 lemon wedges (optional)

Here catfish is sprinkled with seasoned cornmeal and broiled, giving it lots of flavor and a nice crust with just a tiny bit of oil. Whitefish fillets can be substituted for the catfish. Follow this dish with the refreshing Yogurt with Walnuts & Figs (page 132).

Preheat the broiler and position the broiler pan 4–6 inches from the heat.

In a small bowl, combine the cornmeal, paprika, thyme, cayenne, and black pepper and mix well. Set aside.

Arrange the catfish fillets on the broiler pan. Brush the fillets with the oil. Sprinkle the cornmeal mixture evenly over the fish. Broil until the topping is golden brown and the fish is opaque throughout when tested in the center with the tip of a sharp knife, 6–8 minutes. Serve immediately, with the lemon wedges, if using.

NUTRIENT ANALYSIS FOR ONE SERVING

Calories 145	**Calories from Carbs** 13%	**Total Fat** 4 g
Calories from Fat 29%	**Carbohydrates** 5 g	**Saturated Fat** 1 g
Protein 20 g	**Fiber** 0 g	**Monounsaturated Fat** 2 g
Cholesterol 52 mg	**Sugars** 0 g	**Polyunsaturated Fat** 1 g

SOY-GLAZED SALMON WITH GARLIC SPINACH

SERVES 4

Salmon and spinach are a classic nutrient-rich pairing. Look for the lowest-sodium version of soy sauce you can find; you'll still get flavorful results but you'll also get marks for heart health. Lemon-Rice Soup (page 43) is a good starter for this meal.

Place the sesame seeds in a small, dry, nonstick frying pan over medium-high heat. Cook, stirring often, until lightly toasted, 3–5 minutes. Transfer to a plate to cool and set aside.

Prepare a fire in a charcoal grill or preheat a gas grill or oven broiler. Position the grill rack or broiler pan 4–6 inches from the heat source.

Brush the soy sauce over the top of the salmon fillets. Grill or broil, without turning, until the fish is opaque throughout when tested in the center with the tip of a knife, 6–8 minutes.

While the salmon is grilling, place the spinach in a colander and rinse under cold water. Shake off the excess water, but do not dry the spinach. Coat the inside of a large saucepan or Dutch oven with cooking spray and place over medium-high heat. Add the garlic and sauté for 1 minute. Add half of the spinach, cover, and cook, stirring frequently, until the spinach is wilted, about 1 minute. Add the remaining spinach, using tongs to turn the fresh spinach under the wilted spinach. Cover and cook until all the spinach is just wilted, about 1 minute longer. Drain any remaining water.

Divide the spinach among individual plates and top each portion with a salmon fillet. Garnish with the toasted sesame seeds and serve.

1 teaspoon sesame seeds

1½ tablespoons low-sodium soy sauce

4 skinless salmon fillets, about 5 oz each

5 cups firmly packed baby spinach or torn spinach leaves

Cooking spray

2 cloves garlic, minced

NUTRIENT ANALYSIS FOR ONE SERVING

Calories 241	**Calories from Carbs** 14%	**Total Fat** 9 g
Calories from Fat 35%	**Carbohydrates** 9 g	**Saturated Fat** 1 g
Protein 30 g	**Fiber** 3 g	**Monounsaturated Fat** 3 g
Cholesterol 78 mg	**Sugars** 0 g	**Polyunsaturated Fat** 4 g

GRILLED LEMON TROUT

SERVES 4

Cooking spray

4 cleaned and boned whole trout
   or small striped bass, about
   6 oz each

2 tablespoons fresh lemon juice

1 tablespoon chopped fresh thyme
   leaves or 1 teaspoon dried thyme

½ teaspoon freshly ground pepper

2 teaspoons finely shredded lemon
   zest (page 139)

Have your fish market prepare the whole fish for this dish. Both trout and striped bass reach doneness quickly, so watch carefully to avoid overcooking the delicate flesh. Serve with crusty whole-grain rolls or salad.

Prepare a fire in a charcoal grill or preheat a gas grill or oven broiler. Away from the heat source, lightly spray the grill rack or broiler pan with cooking spray. Position the grill rack or broiler pan 4–6 inches from the heat source.

Open each trout flat like a book. Sprinkle the lemon juice, thyme, and pepper evenly over the flesh. Place the trout, skin side down, on the grill rack or broiler pan. Grill or broil until opaque throughout when tested in the center with the tip of a knife, 6–8 minutes. Transfer the trout to warmed individual plates, sprinkle with the lemon zest, and serve immediately.

NUTRIENT ANALYSIS FOR ONE SERVING

Calories 200	**Calories from Carbs** 2%	**Total Fat** 8 g
Calories from Fat 35%	**Carbohydrates** 1 g	**Saturated Fat** 2 g
Protein 30 g	**Fiber** 0 g	**Monounsaturated Fat** 2 g
Cholesterol 90 mg	**Sugars** 0 g	**Polyunsaturated Fat** 2 g

3g

PAN-SEARED SCALLOPS WITH GARLIC & BASIL

SERVES 4

16 large sea scallops, about 1¼ lb total weight

2 teaspoons olive oil

2 cloves garlic, minced

¼ teaspoon freshly ground pepper

2 tablespoons julienned fresh basil or chopped fresh parsley

Don't crowd the scallops in the frying pan, or they will steam instead of sear; cook them in two batches if needed. To julienne fresh herbs, arrange the leaves in a stack, roll the stack length-wise, and slice the roll into thin ribbons.

Pat the scallops dry on paper towels. In a large nonstick frying pan, heat the olive oil over medium-high heat until hot. Add the scallops in a single layer. Sprinkle the garlic and pepper over the scallops and cook, turning once, until opaque throughout when tested in the center with the tip of a knife, about 4 minutes per side. Transfer to a bowl and toss gently with the basil. Arrange on warmed individual plates and serve immediately.

NUTRIENT ANALYSIS FOR ONE SERVING

Calories 149	**Calories from Carbs** 11%	**Total Fat** 3 g
Calories from Fat 22%	**Carbohydrates** 4 g	**Saturated Fat** 0 g
Protein 24 g	**Fiber** 0 g	**Monounsaturated Fat** 2 g
Cholesterol 48 mg	**Sugars** 0 g	**Polyunsaturated Fat** 1 g

BAKED RED SNAPPER WITH MEXICAN SPICES

SERVES 4

4 skinless red snapper fillets, about 4 oz each

2 teaspoons olive oil

1 teaspoon chili powder

1 teaspoon ground cumin

¼ teaspoon cayenne pepper

2 tablespoons chopped fresh cilantro (optional)

4 lime wedges

Pair this tasty, quick-cooking dish with simple steamed green beans or asparagus; the traditional Mexican spices provide plenty of punch. If you don't like cilantro, use fresh parsley instead. Codfish fillets can be used in place of the snapper.

Preheat the oven to 375°F.

Arrange the snapper fillets in a shallow baking dish large enough to hold them in a single layer. Brush the fillets with the olive oil.

In a small bowl, combine the chili powder, cumin, and cayenne and sprinkle the mixture evenly over the fish. Bake until the fillets are opaque throughout when tested in the center with the tip of a knife, 8–10 minutes. Sprinkle with the cilantro, if using, and serve with the lime wedges.

NUTRIENT ANALYSIS FOR ONE SERVING

Calories 120	**Calories from Carbs** 3%	**Total Fat** 3 g
Calories from Fat 26%	**Carbohydrates** 1 g	**Saturated Fat** 0 g
Protein 21 g	**Fiber** 0 g	**Monounsaturated Fat** 2 g
Cholesterol 42 mg	**Sugars** 0 g	**Polyunsaturated Fat** 1 g

MEDITERRANEAN HALIBUT

FAT COUNT 2 g

SODIUM PER SERVING

181 mg   daily limit 2300 mg

SERVES 4

To seed tomatoes, cut them in half crosswise, hold each half over a bowl, and squeeze and shake gently to dislodge the seeds. Serve this flavorful fish dish with Broccoli with Toasted Bread Crumbs (page 106).

Prepare a fire in a charcoal grill or preheat a gas grill or oven broiler. Position the grill rack or broiler pan 4–6 inches from the heat source.

In a small bowl, stir together the vinegar and garlic. Transfer 1 teaspoon of the mixture to another small bowl. Brush the remaining vinegar mixture over the halibut fillets. Sprinkle the fillets with the pepper.

Add the tomato, basil, olives, and olive oil to the reserved vinegar mixture, toss lightly to mix, and set aside while grilling the fish.

Arrange the fish on the grill rack or broiler pan and grill, turning once, until opaque throughout when tested in the center with the tip of a knife, 3–4 minutes per side. Transfer to individual plates and spoon some of the tomato mixture over each portion. Serve immediately.

1 tablespoon balsamic vinegar

2 cloves garlic, minced

4 skinless halibut fillets, about 5 oz each

¼ teaspoon freshly ground pepper

1 ripe tomato, seeded (see note) and chopped

¼ cup chopped fresh basil or parsley

8 Kalamata olives, pitted and chopped

2 teaspoons extra-virgin olive oil

NUTRIENT ANALYSIS FOR ONE SERVING

Calories 210	**Calories from Carbs** 68%	**Total Fat** 2 g
Calories from Fat 18%	**Carbohydrates** 18 g	**Saturated Fat** 0 g
Protein 4 g	**Fiber** 3 g	**Monounsaturated Fat** 1 g
Cholesterol 0 mg	**Sugars** 3 g	**Polyunsaturated Fat** 0 g

SODIUM PER SERVING

110 mg — daily limit 2300 mg

LEMON-GARLIC CHICKEN SKEWERS

SERVES 4

¾ cup low-fat plain yogurt

1 teaspoon paprika, preferably sweet Hungarian

2 cloves garlic, minced

¾ teaspoon finely shredded or grated lemon zest (page 139)

⅛ teaspoon cayenne pepper

1 lb skinless, boneless chicken breasts, cut lengthwise into ¾-inch strips

Four 12-inch metal or presoaked wooden skewers

2 tablespoons chopped fresh cilantro or parsley

This recipe is streamlined by making the marinade and the sauce at the same time. Straining the yogurt is optional, but it thickens the dipping sauce. Soak wooden skewers for about 30 minutes before grilling or broiling to prevent burning.

In a small bowl, combine the yogurt, paprika, garlic, lemon zest, and cayenne and stir to mix well. Transfer ⅓ cup of the yogurt mixture to a paper towel–lined strainer placed over a bowl. Refrigerate while preparing the chicken.

Thread the chicken strips accordion style onto the skewers. Place the skewers on a large, rimmed baking sheet or in a large jelly-roll pan and spoon the remaining yogurt mixture over the chicken, turning to coat both sides. Let marinate at room temperature for 10 minutes.

While the chicken is marinating, preheat the broiler. Place the pan with the skewers under the broiler 4–6 inches from the heat source. Broil, turning once, until the chicken is opaque throughout when tested in the center with the tip of a sharp knife, 4–5 minutes per side. Transfer the skewers to individual plates and sprinkle with the cilantro. Serve with the drained seasoned yogurt for dipping.

NUTRIENT ANALYSIS FOR ONE SERVING

Calories 157	**Calories from Carbs** 2%	**Total Fat** 2 g
Calories from Fat 11%	**Carbohydrates** 5 g	**Saturated Fat** 1 g
Protein 29 g	**Fiber** 0 g	**Monounsaturated Fat** .5 g
Cholesterol 69 mg	**Sugars** 3 g	**Polyunsaturated Fat** .5 g

CHINESE CHICKEN SALAD

SERVES 4

12 oz skinless, boneless chicken breasts

½ cup fat-free, no-salt-added chicken broth

2 tablespoons apricot preserves

2 tablespoons rice vinegar or white wine vinegar

1½ tablespoons low-sodium soy sauce

1½ tablespoons dark sesame oil

1 teaspoon peeled and grated fresh ginger

1 ripe mango

8 cups mesclun or torn mixed salad greens

¼ cup thinly sliced green onion or chopped fresh cilantro

2 teaspoons sesame seeds, toasted (page 61)

Any cooked skinless chicken breast can be used in place of the poached chicken in this simple, elegant main-dish salad. A large navel orange, peeled and diced, may replace the mango. Finish the meal with Broiled Nectarines (page 131).

In a frying pan or saucepan large enough to hold the chicken in a single layer, combine the chicken and broth. Bring to a boil over high heat. Reduce the heat to medium-low, cover, and simmer, turning as needed, until the chicken is opaque throughout when tested in the center with the tip of a sharp knife, about 10 minutes. Transfer the chicken to a cutting board and let stand until cool enough to handle. Reserve the broth for another use. Cut the chicken into strips or shred with your fingers.

While the chicken is poaching, in a small bowl, whisk together the apricot preserves, vinegar, soy sauce, sesame oil, and ginger.

Stand the mango on one of its narrowest ends. Cut the mango off-center, just grazing one side of the pit. Repeat on the other side. Score the cut side of each lobe 4 times vertically and 4 times horizontally (to create a crosshatch), without piercing the peel. Press the mango lobes inside out and slice off the diced fruit near the peel.

Divide the salad greens among individual plates and arrange the chicken, diced mango, and green onion on top. Spoon the dressing over the salads and garnish with the toasted sesame seeds.

NUTRIENT ANALYSIS FOR ONE SERVING

Calories 233	**Calories from Carbs** 34%	**Total Fat** 7 g
Calories from Fat 29%	**Carbohydrates** 20 g	**Saturated Fat** 1 g
Protein 22 g	**Fiber** 3 g	**Monounsaturated Fat** 2 g
Cholesterol 49 mg	**Sugars** 8 g	**Polyunsaturated Fat** 2 g

ROASTED DUCK BREASTS WITH RED WINE SAUCE

SERVES 6

Scoring the skin and searing duck breasts skin side down renders the fat and keeps the meat from drying out during cooking. After the skin and fat are discarded, duck breast is surprisingly lean—even leaner than chicken breasts.

Preheat the oven to 400°F. Score the skin of the duck breasts in a crisscross pattern, being careful not to cut into the duck meat. Heat a large ovenproof, nonstick frying pan over medium heat until very hot. Add the duck, skin side down. Sprinkle the thyme and pepper over the skinless sides of the breasts. Cook until the fat is rendered and the skin is browned, about 10 minutes.

Transfer the duck to a plate and pour off the drippings from the pan. Return the duck to the pan, skin side up. Transfer the pan to the oven and roast the duck until the internal temperature of the thick part of the breasts registers 155°F on an instant-read thermometer. Transfer to a carving board, tent with aluminum foil, and let stand while making the sauce (the internal temperature of the duck will rise to about 160°F while it rests).

Place the pan with the drippings over medium-high heat and whisk in the oil and flour. Cook for 30 seconds. Add the broth and wine and bring to a boil, stirring with a wooden spoon to scrape up any browned bits. Boil gently until the sauce is thickened and reduced by half, about 5 minutes.

Discard the skin from the duck and carve the breasts across the grain on the diagonal into thin slices. Transfer to warmed individual plates and top with the sauce.

4 boneless duck breasts, each about 7 oz each, thawed in the refrigerator if frozen

1 teaspoon dried thyme

½ teaspoon freshly ground pepper

1 tablespoon olive oil

1 tablespoon all-purpose flour

1 cup fat-free, no-salt-added chicken broth

½ cup red wine, port, or fat-free, no-salt-added beef broth

NUTRIENT ANALYSIS FOR ONE SERVING

Calories 182	**Calories from Carbs** 10%	**Total Fat** 4 g
Calories from Fat 23%	**Carbohydrates** 4 g	**Saturated Fat** 1 g
Protein 25 g	**Fiber** 0 g	**Monounsaturated Fat** 3 g
Cholesterol 122 mg	**Sugars** 2 g	**Polyunsaturated Fat** 0 g

CHICKEN PROVENÇAL

SERVES 4

½ teaspoon dried basil

½ teaspoon dried rosemary, crushed

½ teaspoon dried thyme

¼ teaspoon freshly ground pepper

4 skinless, boneless chicken breasts, about 4 oz each

1 tablespoon olive oil

3 large cloves garlic, thinly sliced

2 large tomatoes, seeded (page 67) and chopped

1 tablespoon drained capers

2 anchovy fillets, drained and chopped

Imported ingredients such as capers (the marinated unopened flower buds of a Mediterranean shrub) and anchovy fillets add a richness of flavor and help give this country French dish a distinctive flair.

Sprinkle the basil, rosemary, thyme, and pepper over the chicken. In a large nonstick frying pan, heat the olive oil over medium heat. Add the chicken and cook, without turning, for 5 minutes. Turn the chicken and add the garlic to the pan. Cook, stirring often, for 3 minutes. Add the tomatoes, capers, and anchovies and cook, stirring occasionally and turning the chicken as needed, until the chicken is opaque throughout when tested in the center with the tip of a sharp knife, about 3 minutes longer.

Transfer the chicken to individual plates, top each portion with some of the tomato mixture from the pan, and serve.

NUTRIENT ANALYSIS FOR ONE SERVING

Calories 183	**Calories from Carbs** 11%	**Total Fat** 5 g
Calories from Fat 27%	**Carbohydrates** 5 g	**Saturated Fat** 1 g
Protein 28 g	**Fiber** 1 g	**Monounsaturated Fat** 3 g
Cholesterol 67 mg	**Sugars** 2 g	**Polyunsaturated Fat** 1 g

BRAISED CHICKEN WITH DRIED PLUMS & ALMONDS

FAT COUNT

7 g

SODIUM PER SERVING

222 mg   daily limit 2300 mg

SERVES 4

Dark-meat chicken thighs are moist and flavorful, and slow cooking gives them falling-off-the-bone tenderness. Here the braising time allows dried plums to become plump and soft and contribute to a rich, savory-sweet sauce.

Trim off any excess fat from the chicken. In a small bowl, stir together the paprika, dried sage, and pepper; rub the mixture over the top of the thighs.

Coat the inside of a large nonstick frying pan with cooking spray and heat over medium heat until hot. Add the chicken, seasoned side down. Cook until the seasoned sides are nicely browned, 6–8 minutes. Turn the thighs and add the broth and dried plums to the pan. Bring to a simmer, cover, and cook until the chicken is opaque throughout, about 15 minutes.

Transfer 2 thighs to each individual plate. Spoon the sauce from the pan over the chicken and top with the almonds and fresh sage.

8 skinless, bone-in chicken thighs, about 6 oz each

2 teaspoons paprika

1 teaspoon dried sage

½ teaspoon freshly ground pepper

Olive oil cooking spray

1 cup fat-free, no-salt-added chicken broth

1 cup coarsely chopped dried plums (prunes)

1½ tablespoons sliced unblanched almonds, toasted (page 139)

1½ tablespoons chopped fresh sage or parsley

NUTRIENT ANALYSIS FOR ONE SERVING

Calories 298	**Calories from Carbs** 38%	**Total Fat** 7 g
Calories from Fat 21%	**Carbohydrates** 27 g	**Saturated Fat** 2 g
Protein 30 g	**Fiber** 3 g	**Monounsaturated Fat** 2 g
Cholesterol 115 mg	**Sugars** 13 g	**Polyunsaturated Fat** 2 g

FAT COUNT **10**g

SODIUM PER SERVING

151 mg   daily limit 2300 mg

BEEF & VEGETABLE FAJITAS

SERVES 4

1 teaspoon ground cumin

¼ teaspoon cayenne pepper

¼ teaspoon freshly ground black pepper

1 tomato, seeded (page 67) and chopped

¼ cup thinly sliced green onion

2 tablespoons chopped fresh cilantro (optional)

Cooking spray

1 lb beef top sirloin steak, 1 inch thick, trimmed of visible fat and cut across the grain into thin strips

3 cloves garlic, minced

1 large green bell pepper, seeded and cut into strips

8 corn tortillas, 6 inches in diameter, warmed in a low oven or according to package directions

The lean cut of beef used in this Southwestern-themed dish is a protein-rich option with a relatively small amount of saturated fat. For a more colorful presentation, use a combination of green, red, and yellow bell peppers.

In a bowl, stir together the cumin, cayenne, and black pepper. Set aside 1 teaspoon of the mixture. Add the tomato, green onion, and cilantro, if desired, to the bowl. Toss well and set aside the salsa.

Coat the inside of a large nonstick frying pan with cooking spray and heat over medium-high heat until hot. Add the beef, garlic, and reserved spice mixture to the pan. Cook, tossing continuously, until the beef is barely pink in the center, about 2 minutes. Transfer to a plate and set aside. Add the bell pepper to the pan and cook, tossing continuously, until tender-crisp, about 2 minutes longer. Return the beef to the pan and toss for about 30 seconds.

Serve the beef mixture in the tortillas, topped with the tomato salsa.

NUTRIENT ANALYSIS FOR ONE SERVING

Calories 299	**Calories from Carbs** 39%	**Total Fat** 10 g
Calories from Fat 29%	**Carbohydrates** 29 g	**Saturated Fat** 3 g
Protein 24 g	**Fiber** 4 g	**Monounsaturated Fat** 3 g
Cholesterol 55 mg	**Sugars** 2 g	**Polyunsaturated Fat** 1 g

9 g

GARLIC STEAK & POLENTA

SERVES 4

3 cloves garlic, minced

¼ teaspoon freshly ground pepper

1 lb beef top sirloin steak, 1 inch thick, trimmed of visible fat

1¾ cups fat-free, no-salt-added chicken broth

¾ cup instant polenta or yellow cornmeal

2 tablespoons chopped fresh parsley, thyme, or rosemary

Grilling gives steak terrific flavor, but this dish can also be made using the broiler or a nonstick ridged grill pan; for the grill pan, preheat the pan over medium-high heat until hot and cook the steak for 4–5 minutes per side.

Prepare a fire in a charcoal grill or preheat a gas grill or oven broiler. Position the grill rack or broiler pan 4–6 inches from the heat source.

Sprinkle the garlic and pepper over the steak. Place the steak on the grill rack or broiler pan and cook, turning once, to the desired doneness, 4 minutes per side for medium-rare. Transfer to a carving board, tent with aluminum foil, and let stand for 5 minutes.

While the steak is cooking, combine the broth and polenta in a heavy saucepan and bring to a boil over high heat. Reduce the heat to medium-low and simmer, uncovered, stirring often, until the polenta is very thick, about 6 minutes.

Spoon the polenta onto individual plates. Carve the steak across the grain on the diagonal into thin strips. Arrange the strips over the polenta and drizzle any juices from the carving board over the steak. Garnish with the parsley and serve.

NUTRIENT ANALYSIS FOR ONE SERVING

Calories 288	**Calories from Carbs** 30%	**Total Fat** 9 g
Calories from Fat 28%	**Carbohydrates** 21 g	**Saturated Fat** 3 g
Protein 29 g	**Fiber** 2 g	**Monounsaturated Fat** 4 g
Cholesterol 74 mg	**Sugars** 0 g	**Polyunsaturated Fat** 1 g

DIJON-ORANGE PORK CHOPS

FAT COUNT

3g

SODIUM PER SERVING

395 mg   daily limit 2300 mg

SERVES 4

Rye bread crumbs combine with Dijon mustard and orange juice and zest to give these succulent pork chops loads of flavor. Brown Rice Pilaf with Dates & Almonds (page 111) and Thyme-Scented Mushrooms (page 112) are perfect side dishes.

Place the pork chops in a lock-top plastic bag and add the orange juice. Seal the bag and turn to coat the meat. Refrigerate for at least 15 minutes or up to 2 hours.

While the pork marinates, trim the crusts off the bread slice and tear it into pieces. In a food processor, process the bread to coarse crumbs. Set aside.

Preheat the broiler. Position the broiler pan 4–6 inches from the heat.

Drain the pork chops and discard the orange juice. Place the chops on the broiler pan. Broil for 6 minutes. Turn the chops and broil the second side for 4 minutes. In a small bowl, combine the mustard and orange zest. Remove the chops from the broiler. Brush the mustard mixture over the chops and sprinkle evenly with the bread crumbs. Return to the broiler and broil until the bread crumbs are golden brown and the chops are barely pink in the center, 2–3 minutes longer. Serve immediately.

- 4 boneless, center-cut pork loin chops, about 4 oz each, trimmed of visible fat
- ½ cup fresh orange juice
- 1 slice rye bread
- 1½ tablespoons coarse-grained Dijon mustard
- 1 teaspoon finely grated orange zest (page 139)

NUTRIENT ANALYSIS FOR ONE SERVING

Calories 162	**Calories from Carbs** 15%	**Total Fat** 3 g
Calories from Fat 16%	**Carbohydrates** 6 g	**Saturated Fat** 1 g
Protein 27 g	**Fiber** 1 g	**Monounsaturated Fat** 1 g
Cholesterol 62 mg	**Sugars** 1 g	**Polyunsaturated Fat** 0 g

PORK TENDERLOIN WITH APPLE-SAGE STUFFING

SERVES 4

1 lb pork tenderloin, trimmed of visible fat

⅓ cup diced dried apples

1 slice multigrain bread, cut into ¼-inch cubes

1 tablespoon chopped fresh sage or 1 teaspoon dried sage

½ cup plus 3 tablespoons unsweetened apple juice

¼ teaspoon freshly ground pepper

Cooking spray

This nutritious, comforting dish is pretty to look at and produces an exquisite mingling of flavors. You can find dried apples in well-stocked markets and natural food stores.

Preheat the oven to 375°F. Cut the tenderloin in half lengthwise, being careful not to cut all the way through. Open the tenderloin flat like a book. In a bowl, combine the apples, bread cubes, sage, and the 3 tablespoons apple juice. Spoon the mixture over the tenderloin. Close the tenderloin around the stuffing. To secure the stuffed tenderloin, tie it crosswise with kitchen string every 2 inches. Sprinkle with the pepper.

Coat the inside of a large ovenproof, nonstick frying pan with cooking spray and heat over medium-high heat until hot. Add the tenderloin and cook, rolling it one-quarter turn after each minute of cooking, until well browned on all sides, 3–4 minutes. Transfer the pan to the oven and roast until the internal temperature of the pork registers 150°F on an instant-read thermometer, 12–14 minutes. Transfer the tenderloin to a carving board, tent with aluminum foil, and let stand for 5 minutes (the internal temperature of the pork will rise to about 155°F while it rests).

Place the pan with the drippings over medium heat and add the ½ cup apple juice. Bring to a boil. Cook, stirring with a wooden spoon to scrape up any browned bits, until the sauce is reduced by half, about 2 minutes.

To serve, remove and discard the kitchen string and carve the tenderloin across the grain on the diagonal into 8 slices. Arrange 2 slices on each individual plate and drizzle with the pan sauce.

NUTRIENT ANALYSIS FOR ONE SERVING

Calories 230	**Calories from Carbs** 30%	**Total Fat** 6 g
Calories from Fat 25%	**Carbohydrates** 17 g	**Saturated Fat** 2 g
Protein 26 g	**Fiber** 2 g	**Monounsaturated Fat** 3 g
Cholesterol 63 mg	**Sugars** 11 g	**Polyunsaturated Fat** 1 g

5g

PORK CUTLETS WITH CUMIN & LIME

SERVES 4

2 teaspoons canola oil or olive oil

4 boneless, center-cut pork loin chops, about 4 oz each, trimmed of visible fat

1 teaspoon ground cumin

¼ teaspoon cayenne pepper

½ cup fat-free, no-salt-added chicken broth

4 lime wedges

Cumin and cayenne give ordinary pork chops a depth of flavor. Squeezing the lime juice over the hot chops gives them a clean, fresh taste popular in the Southwest. Serve this quick-cooking pork dish with Roasted Acorn Squash (page 103).

In a large, heavy, nonstick frying pan, heat the oil over medium heat until hot. Add the pork chops. Sprinkle the cumin and cayenne over the chops. Cook, turning once, until barely pink in the center, 4–5 minutes per side. Transfer to warmed individual plates.

Add the broth to the pan and raise the heat to high. Bring to a boil and cook, stirring with a wooden spoon to scrape up any browned bits, until reduced by half, about 2 minutes. Pour the sauce over the chops and serve with the lime wedges.

NUTRIENT ANALYSIS FOR ONE SERVING

Calories 160	**Calories from Carbs** 2%	**Total Fat** 5 g
Calories from Fat 30%	**Carbohydrates** 1 g	**Saturated Fat** 1 g
Protein 26 g	**Fiber** 0 g	**Monounsaturated Fat** 2 g
Cholesterol 62 mg	**Sugars** 0 g	**Polyunsaturated Fat** 1 g

VEAL SCALOPPINE

SERVES 4

Gremolata, the traditional Italian garnish for osso buco, complements other veal dishes as well. A combination of garlic, parsley, and lemon zest, it imparts lively flavor as the heat from the finished dish releases the oils in the ingredients.

In a plastic or paper bag, combine the flour, Parmesan, oregano, and pepper. Add the veal cutlets to the bag one at a time, shaking to coat.

In a large nonstick frying pan, heat 1 teaspoon of the olive oil over medium-high heat. Add half of the veal cutlets and cook, turning once, until lightly browned on both sides, about 2 minutes per side. Transfer to a warmed serving platter and tent with aluminum foil. Repeat with the remaining 1 teaspoon olive oil and the remaining veal cutlets, adding them to the serving platter.

In the same frying pan over medium heat, add the garlic and sauté until fragrant, about 30 seconds. Add the broth and bring to a simmer. Cook, stirring with a wooden spoon to scrape up any browned bits, until the sauce thickens slightly, about 2 minutes.

To make the *gremolata,* in a small bowl, stir together the parsley, garlic, and lemon zest. Pour the pan sauce over the cutlets and top with the *gremolata.*

2 tablespoons all-purpose flour

1½ tablespoons finely grated Parmesan cheese

1½ teaspoons dried oregano

¼ teaspoon freshly ground pepper

1 lb veal cutlets (scaloppine), ¼ inch thick

2 teaspoons olive oil

2 cloves garlic, minced

½ cup fat-free, no-salt-added chicken broth

For the gremolata

2 tablespoons finely chopped fresh parsley

1 small clove garlic, minced

½ teaspoon grated lemon zest (page 139)

NUTRIENT ANALYSIS FOR ONE SERVING

Calories 164	**Calories from Carbs** 10%	**Total Fat** 4 g
Calories from Fat 24%	**Carbohydrates** 4 g	**Saturated Fat** 1 g
Protein 26 g	**Fiber** 0 g	**Monounsaturated Fat** 2 g
Cholesterol 66 mg	**Sugars** 0 g	**Polyunsaturated Fat** 1 g

LAMB STEW WITH NEW POTATOES, PEAS & MINT

SODIUM PER SERVING

126 mg   daily limit 2300 mg

SERVES 6

If you prefer, use lean beef in place of the lamb and substitute chopped fresh thyme or parsley for the mint in this nourishing, flavorful stew. Start the meal with Greek Salad (page 46).

In a large, heavy saucepan, heat the olive oil over medium heat. In a plastic or paper bag, combine the flour and pepper. Add the lamb to the bag, shaking to coat. Transfer to the hot oil and cook, stirring occasionally, until the lamb is beginning to brown on all sides, about 5 minutes. Stir in the onion and garlic and cook, stirring, for 5 minutes longer.

Add the broth, cover, and simmer for 40 minutes. Stir in the potatoes, return to a simmer, and cook, covered, until the lamb and potatoes are tender, 20–25 minutes. Stir in the peas and mint and cook just until the peas are heated through, 3–5 minutes. Ladle into shallow individual bowls and serve.

1 tablespoon olive oil or canola oil

3 tablespoons all-purpose flour

¾ teaspoon freshly ground pepper

1 lb lean lamb stew meat, cut into 1-inch cubes

1 large yellow onion, cut into ½-inch chunks

3 cloves garlic, minced

2½ cups fat-free, no-salt-added beef broth

1 lb red potatoes, scrubbed and cut into 1-inch chunks

1 cup shelled English peas or thawed frozen green peas

2 tablespoons chopped fresh mint

NUTRIENT ANALYSIS FOR ONE SERVING

Calories 244	**Calories from Carbs** 42%	**Total Fat** 7 g
Calories from Fat 25%	**Carbohydrates** 26 g	**Saturated Fat** 2 g
Protein 20 g	**Fiber** 3 g	**Monounsaturated Fat** 3 g
Cholesterol 49 mg	**Sugars** 4 g	**Polyunsaturated Fat** 1 g

6g

SPAGHETTI WITH TOMATOES & SHRIMP

SERVES 4

8 oz dried whole-wheat or 50-percent whole-wheat spaghetti

1 tablespoon olive oil

¾ lb medium shrimp, peeled and deveined

3 cloves garlic, minced

Two 14½-oz cans no-salt-added whole tomatoes, with juice, coarsely chopped

3 tablespoons tomato paste

1 tablespoon chopped fresh basil or 1 teaspoon dried basil

1 tablespoon chopped fresh oregano or 1 teaspoon dried oregano

1 tablespoon drained capers

¼ teaspoon red pepper flakes

Chopped fresh basil for garnish (optional)

For easy chopping, use kitchen scissors to cut large pieces of tomatoes into chunks right in the can. Look for tomato paste in a tube for convenient storage of leftover paste. If using frozen shrimp, thaw them under cold running water before peeling.

Bring a saucepan three-fourths full of water to a boil. Add the spaghetti and cook until al dente, 8–10 minutes.

Meanwhile, in a large saucepan, heat the olive oil over medium heat. Add the shrimp and garlic and sauté until the shrimp are opaque throughout, about 4 minutes. Transfer the mixture to a bowl and set aside.

Add the tomatoes, tomato paste, basil, oregano, capers, and red pepper flakes to the pan. Bring to a simmer and cook, uncovered, stirring occasionally, for 10 minutes. Return the shrimp mixture to the pan and cook until heated through, about 2 minutes.

Drain the spaghetti and divide among warmed individual plates. Top with the tomato-shrimp sauce and sprinkle with chopped basil, if using.

NUTRIENT ANALYSIS FOR ONE SERVING

Calories 347	**Calories from Carbs** 55%	**Total Fat** 6 g
Calories from Fat 15%	**Carbohydrates** 48 g	**Saturated Fat** 1 g
Protein 26 g	Fiber 7 g	**Monounsaturated Fat** 3 g
Cholesterol 129 mg	Sugars 10 g	**Polyunsaturated Fat** 1 g

GRILLED PORTOBELLO SANDWICHES

FAT COUNT

9 g

SODIUM PER SERVING

369 mg   daily limit 2300 mg

SERVES 4

Extra large and juicy, portobello mushrooms are meaty enough to satisfy anyone's urge for a hamburger. This open-faced sandwich is perfect for the summer months when bell peppers are at their peak. Start with Fresh Corn Salad (page 45).

Prepare a fire in a charcoal grill or preheat a gas grill or oven broiler. Away from the heat source, lightly spray the grill rack or broiler pan with cooking spray. Position the grill rack or broiler pan 4–6 inches from the heat source.

In a small bowl, whisk together the olive oil and vinegar. Brush the mixture over both sides of the mushrooms and the bell pepper halves. Arrange the mushrooms and peppers on the grill or broiler pan and grill, covered, or broil until tender, 4–5 minutes per side.

Place a slice of toast on each plate and top each with a mushroom and a bell pepper half. Sprinkle with the feta, season with the pepper, and serve.

Cooking spray

1 tablespoon olive oil

1 tablespoon balsamic vinegar

4 portobello mushrooms, about 4 oz each, stems trimmed

2 large red or yellow bell peppers, halved lengthwise, stemmed, seeded, and deribbed

4 slices multigrain bread, toasted

½ cup crumbled reduced-fat feta or goat cheese

¼ teaspoon freshly ground pepper

NUTRIENT ANALYSIS FOR ONE SERVING

Calories 255	**Calories from Carbs** 52%	**Total Fat** 9 g
Calories from Fat 32%	**Carbohydrates** 34 g	**Saturated Fat** 3 g
Protein 10 g	**Fiber** 6 g	**Monounsaturated Fat** 4 g
Cholesterol 17 mg	**Sugars** 13 g	**Polyunsaturated Fat** 1 g

WHITE BEAN CASSEROLE

SERVES 4

2 tablespoons olive oil

1 yellow onion, chopped

3 cloves garlic, minced

Two 15-oz cans no-salt-added Great Northern beans or navy beans, rinsed and drained

1 large tomato, chopped

1 tablespoon chopped fresh thyme or 1 teaspoon dried thyme

¼ teaspoon freshly ground pepper

3 tablespoons plain dried bread crumbs

This hearty meatless main dish is full of flavor and low-fat protein. The golden brown topping makes an attractive finish. If you like, you can substitute 2 cups cooked dried beans for the canned beans.

Preheat the oven to 375°F.

In a saucepan, heat 1 tablespoon of the olive oil over medium heat. Add the onion and garlic and sauté until softened, about 5 minutes. Remove from the heat and stir in the beans, tomato, thyme, and pepper. Transfer to a shallow 1½-qt gratin dish or an 8-inch square glass baking dish.

In a small bowl, combine the bread crumbs and the remaining 1 tablespoon olive oil and sprinkle over the bean mixture. Bake until the bread crumbs are golden brown, 20–25 minutes. Divide among warmed individual plates and serve.

NUTRIENT ANALYSIS FOR ONE SERVING

Calories 303	**Calories from Carbs** 58%	**Total Fat** 8 g
Calories from Fat 24%	**Carbohydrates** 44 g	**Saturated Fat** 1 g
Protein 14 g	**Fiber** 14 g	**Monounsaturated Fat** 6 g
Cholesterol 0 mg	**Sugars** 3 g	**Polyunsaturated Fat** 1 g

FETTUCCINE WITH FRESH TOMATO SAUCE

FAT COUNT

7 g

SODIUM PER SERVING

148 mg   daily limit 2300 mg

SERVES 4

This meatless pasta dish is a treat when vine-ripened summer tomatoes are in season. Out of season, use hydroponically grown or hothouse tomatoes. You can omit the seeding step if you like; the seeds are removed here for aesthetic reasons only.

Bring a large saucepan three-fourths full of water to a boil. Add the fettuccine and cook until al dente, 8–10 minutes.

Meanwhile, cut the tomatoes in half crosswise. Place a strainer over a bowl and squeeze the seeds and juices from the tomato halves into the strainer. Coarsely chop the tomatoes and set aside. Press on the seeds with the back of a wooden spoon to extract the tomato juices. Discard the seeds and set the juices aside.

In a large frying pan, heat the olive oil over medium heat. Add the garlic and sauté for 2 minutes. Add the tomatoes, tomato juices, basil, vinegar, and red pepper flakes. Cook, stirring once or twice, just until the tomatoes are heated through, 1–2 minutes.

Drain the fettuccine and divide among warmed individual plates. Top with the tomato sauce and the Parmesan.

½ lb dried spinach fettuccine or whole-wheat fettuccine or spaghetti

2 lb very ripe tomatoes

1 tablespoon olive oil

3 cloves garlic, minced

¼ cup chopped fresh basil or parsley

1 tablespoon balsamic vinegar

½ teaspoon red pepper flakes or freshly ground black pepper

¼ cup grated Parmesan cheese

NUTRIENT ANALYSIS FOR ONE SERVING

Calories 182	**Calories from Carbs** 53%	**Total Fat** 7 g
Calories from Fat 31%	**Carbohydrates** 25 g	**Saturated Fat** 2 g
Protein 8 g	**Fiber** 5 g	**Monounsaturated Fat** 3 g
Cholesterol 8 mg	**Sugars** 7 g	**Polyunsaturated Fat** 1 g

BELL PEPPERS STUFFED WITH BEANS & RICE

FAT COUNT

9g

SODIUM PER SERVING

358 mg   daily limit 2300 mg

SERVES 4

This dish is a vegetarian delight. Parboiling the peppers cuts the baking time in half, but be sure to drain them thoroughly before stuffing them. Follow with Pineapple & Mango with Lime (page 128) for dessert.

Preheat the oven to 400°F.

Bring a saucepan three-fourths full of water to a boil. Meanwhile, cut off the stem ends of the peppers, ½ inch from the top. Chop the pepper tops, discarding the stems, and set aside. Remove the seeds and ribs from the peppers to create cups. Add the pepper cups to the boiling water and cook until tender-crisp, 3–4 minutes. Drain well and set aside.

In a saucepan, heat the olive oil over medium heat. Add the chopped pepper tops and the onion and cook, stirring occasionally, for 2 minutes. Add the rice, water, and broth and bring to a simmer. Cover, reduce the heat to medium-low, and simmer for 45 minutes. Turn off the heat and let stand for 5 minutes. Stir in the beans, ½ cup of the feta, and ¼ cup of the cilantro.

Stand the pepper cups upright in a baking dish. Divide the rice mixture among the pepper cups. Cover loosely with aluminum foil and bake until the peppers are tender and the filling is hot throughout, about 20 minutes. Transfer to individual plates and top with the remaining ½ cup of feta and the remaining 2 tablespoons of cilantro.

- 4 large red or yellow bell peppers, or a combination
- 1 tablespoon olive oil
- ½ cup chopped yellow onion
- ⅔ cup long-grain brown rice
- 1 cup water
- ¾ cup fat-free, no-salt-added vegetable or chicken broth
- One 15-oz can no-salt-added black beans, rinsed and drained
- 1 cup crumbled reduced-fat feta cheese
- ¼ cup plus 2 tablespoons chopped fresh cilantro or parsley

NUTRIENT ANALYSIS FOR ONE SERVING

Calories 352	**Calories from Carbs** 59%	**Total Fat** 9 g
Calories from Fat 24%	**Carbohydrates** 3 g	**Saturated Fat** 4 g
Protein 15 g	**Fiber** 11 g	**Monounsaturated Fat** 3 g
Cholesterol 15 mg	**Sugars** 7 g	**Polyunsaturated Fat** 1 g

4g

SPANISH OMELET

SERVES 4

2 teaspoons olive oil

1 yellow onion, quartered and
cut into thin wedges

8 oz small red potatoes, scrubbed
and thinly sliced

½ cup fat-free, no-salt-added
vegetable or chicken broth

¼ teaspoon freshly ground pepper

5 large egg whites

1 large egg

⅓ cup jarred roasted red bell
peppers, drained and diced

2 tablespoons chopped fresh
parsley or basil

This is a light version of the traditional Spanish dish, which
is usually loaded with olive oil. If small red potatoes are not
available, cut larger ones in half, then thinly slice. If your frying
pan is not ovenproof, wrap the handle in heavy aluminum foil.

Preheat the oven to 375°F.

In a 9-inch ovenproof, nonstick frying pan, heat the olive oil over medium-high heat. Add the onion and cook, stirring occasionally, until lightly browned, about 4 minutes. Add the potatoes, broth, and pepper and stir to mix well. Simmer, uncovered, stirring occasionally, until the potatoes are tender and the broth is absorbed, about 10 minutes.

In a bowl, use a whisk or fork to beat together the egg whites and the whole egg. Stir the eggs into the potato mixture, mixing well and patting down with a spatula to compact the omelet. Transfer to the oven and bake until the eggs are set, about 10 minutes.

Meanwhile, in a small bowl, combine the roasted red peppers and parsley. Cut the omelet into 4 wedges and transfer to warmed individual plates. Top with the roasted red pepper mixture and serve.

NUTRIENT ANALYSIS FOR ONE SERVING

Calories 135	**Calories from Carbs** 51%	**Total Fat** 4 g
Calories from Fat 25%	**Carbohydrates** 17 g	**Saturated Fat** 1 g
Protein 8 g	**Fiber** 2 g	**Monounsaturated Fat** 2 g
Cholesterol 47 mg	**Sugars** 4 g	**Polyunsaturated Fat** .5 g

SIDE DISHES

Roasted Beets, 115

GREEN BEANS WITH SHALLOTS & THYME

SERVES 4

¾ lb green beans

2 teaspoons unsalted butter

¼ cup thinly sliced shallots or
   chopped red onion

1 tablespoon chopped fresh thyme
   or 1 teaspoon dried thyme

¼ teaspoon freshly ground pepper

Newer varieties of green beans lack the tough, fibrous string that used to run along their length; all you need to do is trim their stem ends. Available year-round, these family favorites are packed with the antioxidant vitamins A and C.

Preheat the oven to 375°F.

Bring a saucepan three-fourths full of water to a boil. Add the green beans and cook until tender-crisp, about 4 minutes. Drain; transfer to a shallow roasting pan or an 8-inch glass baking dish. Add the butter and toss until melted and the green beans are coated. Add the shallots, thyme, and pepper and toss again. Bake, uncovered, until the beans are tender when pierced with the tip of a sharp knife, about 8 minutes. Serve immediately.

NUTRIENT ANALYSIS FOR ONE SERVING

Calories 64	**Calories from Carbs** 61%	**Total Fat** 2 g
Calories from Fat 25%	**Carbohydrates** 11 g	**Saturated Fat** 1 g
Protein 3 g	**Fiber** 3 g	**Monounsaturated Fat** 1 g
Cholesterol 5 mg	**Sugars** 2 g	**Polyunsaturated Fat** 0 g

ROASTED ACORN SQUASH

FAT COUNT

2 g

SODIUM PER SERVING

16 mg   daily limit 2300 mg

SERVES 4

Acorn squash, a variety of hard-skinned winter squash, is actually available year-round and is an excellent source of iron, riboflavin, and vitamins A and C. This simple side dish gives off a delightfully sweet aroma as it bakes.

Preheat the oven to 375°F.

Cut small squashes in half crosswise or cut large squash into quarters. Using a spoon, scoop out the seeds and any fibers. Sprinkle the nutmeg over the cut sides of the squash pieces.

Pour the apple cider into an 8- or 9-inch square glass baking dish. Arrange the squash pieces, cut side down, in the dish. Bake, uncovered, until the squash is tender and the cider is reduced to about 1/3 cup, 50–55 minutes. Transfer the squash to individual plates. Add the butter to the dish with the remaining cider and stir until melted. Drizzle the sauce over the squash and serve.

2 small or 1 large acorn squash, about 2½ lb

¼ teaspoon freshly grated nutmeg

¾ cup unsweetened apple cider or apple juice

2 teaspoons unsalted butter

NUTRIENT ANALYSIS FOR ONE SERVING

Calories 198	**Calories from Carbs** 85%	**Total Fat** 2 g
Calories from Fat 9%	**Carbohydrates** 47 g	**Saturated Fat** 1 g
Protein 3 g	**Fiber** 5 g	**Monounsaturated Fat** 0 g
Cholesterol 5 mg	**Sugars** 5 g	**Polyunsaturated Fat** 0 g

CREAMY SWISS CHARD

SERVES 4

2 teaspoons unsalted butter

2 cloves garlic, minced

1 lb Swiss chard, thick ribs cut away, leaves and stems thinly sliced

¾ cup fat-free milk

¼ teaspoon freshly ground pepper

⅛ teaspoon freshly grated nutmeg

Any type of Swiss chard will work in this easy recipe, but look for colorful rainbow chard in the organic produce section of the supermarket. The texture of this dish is similar to Southern-style boiled greens, but it gets its creamy flavor from milk.

In a large saucepan, melt the butter over medium heat. Add the garlic and sauté for 1 minute. Add the Swiss chard, milk, pepper, and nutmeg. Cook, tossing often with tongs, until the milk is absorbed and the chard is tender, 12–15 minutes. Serve immediately.

NUTRIENT ANALYSIS FOR ONE SERVING

Calories 57	**Calories from Carbs** 47%	**Total Fat** 2 g
Calories from Fat 28%	**Carbohydrates** 7 g	**Saturated Fat** 1 g
Protein 4 g	**Fiber** 2 g	**Monounsaturated Fat** 0 g
Cholesterol 6 mg	**Sugars** 3 g	**Polyunsaturated Fat** 0 g

HORSERADISH MASHED POTATOES

FAT COUNT 4g

SODIUM PER SERVING

56 mg   daily limit 2300 mg

SERVES 6

Buttermilk lends a tangy flavor to this perennial-favorite side dish. Leaving the skin on the potatoes adds flavor, texture, and fiber. Yukon gold potatoes may be used, but avoid using russet potatoes because the results will be less creamy.

In a saucepan, combine the potatoes with cold water to cover and bring to a simmer over high heat. Cover, reduce the heat to medium-low, and cook until the potatoes are tender, about 15 minutes.

Drain the potatoes well and return to the saucepan over low heat. Using a potato masher, mash the potatoes to the desired consistency, gradually adding the buttermilk. Stir in the horseradish, olive oil, and pepper. Serve immediately.

1½ lb red potatoes, scrubbed and cut into 1-inch chunks

¾ cup low-fat buttermilk

2 tablespoons prepared horseradish

1½ tablespoons olive oil or unsalted butter

¼ teaspoon freshly ground pepper

NUTRIENT ANALYSIS FOR ONE SERVING

Calories 130	**Calories from Carbs** 62%	**Total Fat** 4 g
Calories from Fat 28%	**Carbohydrates** 20 g	**Saturated Fat** 1 g
Protein 3 g	**Fiber** 2 g	**Monounsaturated Fat** 3 g
Cholesterol 2 mg	**Sugars** 3 g	**Polyunsaturated Fat** 0 g

2 g

BROCCOLI WITH TOASTED BREAD CRUMBS

SERVES 4

⅓ cup fat-free, no-salt-added vegetable or chicken broth

1 lb broccoli, trimmed and cut into florets, stems thinly sliced

2 slices multigrain bread

½ teaspoon finely shredded lemon zest (page 139)

1 clove garlic, minced

1½ teaspoons unsalted butter, melted

Cutting the broccoli into florets and thinly slicing the stems allows for more even cooking. Make extra bread crumbs for future use; freeze in a lock-top plastic bag for up to 3 months.

Preheat the oven to 375°F.

In a saucepan over medium heat, bring the broth to a simmer. Add the broccoli and cook until tender-crisp, 3–4 minutes. Transfer to a shallow 1½- to 2-qt casserole dish or 8-inch square baking dish. (Alternatively, combine the broccoli and broth in a shallow, microwave-safe casserole dish or baking dish. Cover with waxed paper and cook in the microwave until the broccoli is tender-crisp, 3–4 minutes.)

Meanwhile, trim the crusts off the bread slices and tear the bread into pieces. In a food processor, process to coarse crumbs.

In a bowl, combine the bread crumbs, lemon zest, and garlic. Sprinkle the crumb mixture evenly over the broccoli. Drizzle the melted butter over the crumb topping. Bake, uncovered, until the broccoli is tender and the bread crumbs are golden brown, 10–12 minutes. Serve immediately.

NUTRIENT ANALYSIS FOR ONE SERVING

Calories 57	**Calories from Carbs** 53%	**Total Fat** 2 g
Calories from Fat 26%	**Carbohydrates** 9 g	**Saturated Fat** 1 g
Protein 3 g	**Fiber** 3 g	**Monounsaturated Fat** 0 g
Cholesterol 4 mg	**Sugars** 2 g	**Polyunsaturated Fat** 0 g

CARROTS WITH ORANGE-CINNAMON BROTH

SERVES 4

FAT COUNT 3 g

SODIUM PER SERVING

83 mg   daily limit 2300 mg

Prepared baby carrots, now widely available, make this dish exceptionally easy to make. Large carrots, peeled and sliced on the diagonal into ½-inch rounds, may be substituted if baby carrots are not available.

In a saucepan, combine the carrots, broth, and orange juice and bring to a simmer over high heat. Reduce the heat to medium-low, cover, and simmer until the carrots are tender, about 14 minutes. Return the heat to high, uncover the pan, and continue to cook until most of the liquid is absorbed. Remove from the heat and stir in the butter and cinnamon until well combined. Garnish with the parsley and serve immediately.

1 lb baby carrots

¼ cup fat-free, no-salt-added vegetable or chicken broth

¼ cup fresh orange juice

1 tablespoon unsalted butter

⅛ teaspoon ground cinnamon

1 tablespoon chopped fresh parsley

NUTRIENT ANALYSIS FOR ONE SERVING

Calories 87	**Calories from Carbs** 64%	**Total Fat** 3 g
Calories from Fat 29%	**Carbohydrates** 14 g	**Saturated Fat** 2 g
Protein 1 g	**Fiber** 3 g	**Monounsaturated Fat** 0 g
Cholesterol 8 mg	**Sugars** 8 g	**Polyunsaturated Fat** 0 g

ROASTED ROOT VEGETABLES

SERVES 4

1 sweet potato, scrubbed and cut into 1-inch chunks

½ lb parsnips, peeled and sliced into ½-inch rounds

½ lb carrots, peeled and sliced into ½-inch rounds

⅔ cup fat-free, no-salt-added vegetable or chicken broth

1 tablespoon olive oil

1 tablespoon chopped fresh thyme or 1 teaspoon dried thyme

¼ teaspoon freshly ground pepper

Of the many types of sweet potato, the two most widely available are the yellow-skinned kind with pale flesh and the variety with red-brown skin and orange flesh. Use dark-skinned sweet potatoes for roasting as they are moister and sweeter.

Preheat the oven to 400°F.

In a large jelly-roll pan or roasting pan, combine the sweet potato, parsnips, carrots, broth, olive oil, thyme, and pepper and toss to coat. Arrange the vegetables in a single layer. Roast for 15 minutes. Remove from the oven and toss well. Return to the oven and continue to roast until the vegetables are glazed and tender, about 15 minutes longer. Serve immediately.

NUTRIENT ANALYSIS FOR ONE SERVING

Calories 163	**Calories from Carbs** 74%	**Total Fat** 4 g
Calories from Fat 20%	**Carbohydrates** 31 g	**Saturated Fat** 1 g
Protein 2 g	**Fiber** 5 g	**Monounsaturated Fat** 3 g
Cholesterol 0 mg	**Sugars** 12 g	**Polyunsaturated Fat** 0 g

BROWN RICE PILAF WITH DATES & ALMONDS

FAT COUNT

3g

SODIUM PER SERVING

135 mg   daily limit 2300 mg

SERVES 6

This hearty side dish is a delicious high-fiber alternative to traditional white-rice pilafs. Aromatic Texmati and brown basmati also complement the Middle Eastern flavors in this dish. Serve with Dijon-Orange Pork Chops (page 81).

In a saucepan, combine the rice and broth and bring to a boil over high heat. Reduce the heat to medium-low, cover, and simmer for 30 minutes. Stir in the dates and continue to simmer, covered, until the liquid is absorbed and the rice is tender, about 10 minutes longer. Remove from the heat and let stand, covered, for 5 minutes. Stir in the almonds and serve.

1 cup long-grain brown rice

2¼ cups fat-free, no-salt-added vegetable or chicken broth

½ cup chopped pitted dates

⅓ cup sliced unblanched almonds, toasted (page 139)

NUTRIENT ANALYSIS FOR ONE SERVING

Calories 179	**Calories from Carbs** 76%	**Total Fat** 3 g
Calories from Fat 16%	**Carbohydrates** 35 g	**Saturated Fat** 0 g
Protein 3 g	**Fiber** 3 g	**Monounsaturated Fat** 2 g
Cholesterol 0 mg	**Sugars** 10 g	**Polyunsaturated Fat** 1 g

THYME-SCENTED MUSHROOMS

SERVES 4

2 teaspoons unsalted butter

⅓ cup chopped shallots or yellow onion

¾ lb cremini or button mushrooms, brushed clean and sliced

1 tablespoon chopped fresh thyme or 1 teaspoon dried thyme

¼ teaspoon freshly ground pepper

½ cup fat-free, no-salt-added vegetable, beef, or chicken broth

Cremini mushrooms are similar in size to button mushrooms, but they have a brown color and an earthier flavor. For a more varied flavor, look for packages of mixed sliced exotic mushrooms (often a mix of oyster, shiitake, and cremini).

In a large nonstick frying pan, melt the butter over medium heat. Add the shallots and sauté for 2 minutes. Add the mushrooms, thyme, and pepper and cook, stirring occasionally, for 2 minutes longer. Add the broth and bring to a simmer. Cook until most of the liquid is absorbed and the mushrooms and shallots are tender, 6–8 minutes. Serve immediately.

NUTRIENT ANALYSIS FOR ONE SERVING

Calories 65	**Calories from Carbs** 58%	**Total Fat** 2 g
Calories from Fat 23%	**Carbohydrates** 11 g	**Saturated Fat** 1 g
Protein 4 g	**Fiber** 1 g	**Monounsaturated Fat** 0 g
Cholesterol 5 mg	**Sugars** 3 g	**Polyunsaturated Fat** 0 g

ROASTED BEETS

SERVES 4

FAT COUNT

3 g

SODIUM PER SERVING

111 mg   daily limit 2300 mg

For a more colorful dish, look for "bull's-eye" chioggia or golden beets at farmers' markets or in the organic produce section of supermarkets. The beets may be prepared up to 1 hour before serving and reheated in a 300°F oven until warm.

Preheat the oven to 400°F.

Place the beets in an 8-inch square baking dish. Drizzle the water over the beets and cover the dish with aluminum foil. Bake until the beets are tender when pierced with the tip of a knife, about 45 minutes. Uncover and let cool in the dish.

When the beets are cool enough to handle, remove the peels with a small, sharp knife. Discard the peels and cut the beets into thin wedges. Arrange the wedges on a serving dish. Drizzle with the olive oil and sprinkle with the pepper. Serve warm or at room temperature.

4 large or 8 medium beets, trimmed and scrubbed

2 tablespoons water

2 teaspoons olive oil

½ teaspoon freshly ground pepper

NUTRIENT ANALYSIS FOR ONE SERVING

Calories 83	**Calories from Carbs** 63%	**Total Fat** 3 g
Calories from Fat 27%	**Carbohydrates** 14 g	**Saturated Fat** 0 g
Protein 2 g	**Fiber** 4 g	**Monounsaturated Fat** 2 g
Cholesterol 0 mg	**Sugars** 10 g	**Polyunsaturated Fat** 0 g

SAUTÉED SQUASH WITH TOMATOES & BASIL

SERVES 4

1 teaspoon olive oil

2 cloves garlic, minced

2 green zucchini, sliced

2 yellow zucchini or crookneck squash, sliced

¼ teaspoon freshly ground pepper

1 large tomato, seeded (page 67) and chopped

2 tablespoons chopped fresh basil or parsley

This colorful, antioxidant-rich dish takes advantage of the seasonal bounty of summer and especially complements Italian-themed meals. It also makes a lovely accompaniment to Spicy Broiled Catfish (page 58).

In a large nonstick frying pan, heat the olive oil over medium heat. Add the garlic and sauté for 30 seconds. Add the squash and the pepper and cook, tossing occasionally, for 2 minutes. Cover, reduce the heat to low, and cook until the squash is tender-crisp, 4–6 minutes. Uncover, stir in the tomato and basil, and cook just until the tomato is heated through, 2–3 minutes longer. Serve immediately.

NUTRIENT ANALYSIS FOR ONE SERVING

Calories 40	**Calories from Carbs** 54%	**Total Fat** 1 g
Calories from Fat 28%	**Carbohydrates** 6 g	**Saturated Fat** 0 g
Protein 2 g	**Fiber** 3 g	**Monounsaturated Fat** 1 g
Cholesterol 0 mg	**Sugars** 1 g	**Polyunsaturated Fat** 0 g

RED LENTILS
& BROWNED ONIONS

SERVES 5

¾ cup low-fat plain yogurt

2½ cups fat-free, no-salt-added vegetable or chicken broth

1 cup dried red lentils

½ teaspoon curry powder

⅛ teaspoon cayenne pepper

2 teaspoons olive oil or canola oil

1 sweet onion such as Vidalia or Walla Walla, quartered and cut into thin wedges

2 tablespoons chopped fresh cilantro or parsley

Small red lentils cook quickly and have a delicious peppery flavor. If unavailable, substitute brown lentils and increase the cooking time to 30 minutes, adding more broth if necessary. Draining the yogurt is optional, but will thicken the garnish.

Spoon the yogurt into a paper towel–lined strainer placed over a bowl. Refrigerate while preparing the lentils.

In a saucepan, combine the broth, lentils, curry powder, and cayenne and bring to a boil over high heat. Reduce the heat to medium and simmer, uncovered, until the lentils are tender and the liquid is absorbed, about 20 minutes.

Meanwhile, in a large nonstick frying pan over medium-high heat, heat the oil. Add the onion wedges and cook, stirring occasionally, until they are a deep golden brown, 7–9 minutes.

Spoon the lentils onto warmed individual plates and top with the onion, yogurt, and cilantro.

NUTRIENT ANALYSIS FOR ONE SERVING

Calories 179	**Calories from Carbs** 64%	**Total Fat** 2 g
Calories from Fat 11%	**Carbohydrates** 29 g	**Saturated Fat** .5 g
Protein 11 g	**Fiber** 6 g	**Monounsaturated Fat** 1.5 g
Cholesterol 2 mg	**Sugars** 6 g	**Polyunsaturated Fat** 0 g

BUTTERMILK CORN MUFFINS

FAT COUNT

2 g

SODIUM PER SERVING

119 mg   daily limit 2300 mg

MAKES 12 MUFFINS

Buttermilk gives these corn muffins a moist texture and replaces the usual large amount of butter or oil. Serve as a side dish or for a delicious and quick snack. Freeze any extra muffins in a lock-top plastic bag for up to 3 months.

Preheat the oven to 425°F. Line a standard 12-cup muffin pan with paper baking cups.

In a bowl, whisk together the cornmeal, flour, baking powder, and baking soda. Add the buttermilk, egg, honey, and oil; mix just until the dry ingredients are moistened. Spoon the batter into the prepared muffin cups. Bake until golden brown and a wooden toothpick inserted into the center of a muffin comes out clean, 12–14 minutes. Serve warm.

1 cup yellow cornmeal

1 cup all-purpose flour

1 teaspoon baking powder

½ teaspoon baking soda

1 cup low-fat buttermilk

1 large egg, lightly beaten

2 tablespoons honey

1 tablespoon canola oil or vegetable oil

NUTRIENT ANALYSIS PER MUFFIN

Calories 123	**Calories from Carbs** 74%	**Total Fat** 2 g
Calories from Fat 16%	**Carbohydrates** 23 g	**Saturated Fat** 0 g
Protein 3 g	**Fiber** 1 g	**Monounsaturated Fat** 1 g
Cholesterol 22 mg	**Sugars** 8 g	**Polyunsaturated Fat** 1 g

DESSERTS & SNACKS

Pineapple & Mango with Lime, 128

3g

STRAWBERRIES WITH ORANGE & ALMOND

SERVES 4

3 cups hulled, sliced strawberries

2 tablespoons fresh orange juice

3 tablespoons sliced unblanched almonds, toasted (page 139)

1 teaspoon finely shredded orange zest (page 139)

Nuts, berries, and citrus combine to bring full flavor to this simple but nutritious dessert. For double orange flavor, add 1 tablespoon Grand Marnier or other orange-flavored liqueur to the strawberries along with the orange juice.

In a bowl, combine the strawberries and orange juice. Toss gently and divide among 4 small dessert bowls. Top with the almonds and orange zest and serve immediately or refrigerate for up to 3 hours.

NUTRIENT ANALYSIS FOR ONE SERVING

Calories 70	**Calories from Carbs** 59%	**Total Fat** 3 g
Calories from Fat 31%	**Carbohydrates** 11 g	**Saturated Fat** 0 g
Protein 2 g	**Fiber** 3 g	**Monounsaturated Fat** 1.5 g
Cholesterol 0 mg	**Sugars** 3 g	**Polyunsaturated Fat** 1 g

PEAR CRUMBLE

SERVES 6

Wheat germ, the seed of the wheat kernel, is a concentrated source of protein, vitamins, and minerals. Look for jars of toasted wheat germ and honey wheat germ in the cereal aisle of well-stocked supermarkets.

Preheat the oven to 375°F.

Arrange the pear slices in slightly overlapping concentric circles in a 9-inch pie dish. Sprinkle 2 tablespoons of the apple juice concentrate evenly over the pears.

In a small bowl, combine the oats, wheat germ, dates, and cinnamon and mix well. Add the remaining 2 tablespoons apple juice concentrate and the canola oil and toss to mix well. Sprinkle the topping over the pears. Bake until the pears are tender and the topping is golden brown, 25–30 minutes. Serve warm or at room temperature.

4 ripe but firm Bartlett (Williams) or Anjou pears, unpeeled, cored and thickly sliced lengthwise

4 tablespoons thawed frozen apple juice concentrate

½ cup old-fashioned rolled oats

⅓ cup toasted wheat germ

¼ cup finely chopped pitted dates

¾ teaspoon ground cinnamon

2 tablespoons canola oil

NUTRIENT ANALYSIS FOR ONE SERVING

Calories 190	**Calories from Carbs** 67%	**Total Fat** 6 g
Calories from Fat 26%	**Carbohydrates** 34 g	**Saturated Fat** 0 g
Protein 3 g	**Fiber** 6 g	**Monounsaturated Fat** 3 g
Cholesterol 0 mg	**Sugars** 20 g	**Polyunsaturated Fat** 2 g

TROPICAL FRUIT SALAD

SERVES 4

Toasted coconut is an easy, healthy, and flavorful addition to this vitamin-packed dessert. Serve this fruit salad after Fettuccine with Fresh Tomato Sauce (page 93). You can substitute orange for the mango, if you like.

⅓ cup shredded coconut

1 ripe mango

1 small ripe banana

2 small kiwifruit

Toast the coconut by spreading it on a baking sheet or toaster-over tray and baking in a 350°F oven, stirring once to prevent burning, until fragrant and lightly browned, about 5 minutes.

Stand the mango on one of its narrowest ends. Cut the mango off-center, just grazing one side of the pit. Repeat on the other side. Score the cut side of each lobe 4 times vertically and 4 times horizontally (to create a crosshatch), without piercing the peel. Press the mango lobes inside out and slice off the diced fruit near the peel.

Peel and slice the banana and the kiwifruit. In a bowl, combine the banana, mango, kiwi, and coconut and toss gently to mix. Serve immediately, or cover and refrigerate for up to 2 hours.

NUTRIENT ANALYSIS FOR ONE SERVING

Calories 118	**Calories from Carbs** 75%	**Total Fat** 3 g
Calories from Fat 23%	**Carbohydrates** 24 g	**Saturated Fat** 2 g
Protein 1 g	**Fiber** 3 g	**Monounsaturated Fat** 0 g
Cholesterol 0 mg	**Sugars** 8 g	**Polyunsaturated Fat** 0 g

SODIUM PER SERVING

5 mg   daily limit 2300 mg

PINEAPPLE & MANGO WITH LIME

SERVES 4

1 small ripe pineapple

1 ripe mango or papaya

2 tablespoons fresh lime juice

¼ teaspoon chili powder

⅛ teaspoon cayenne pepper
  (optional)

To speed up the preparation time for this exotically spiced Mexican snack, purchase a whole cored pineapple, often sold in plastic containers in the supermarket produce section. The optional cayenne pepper will give the dish a hot-sweet flavor.

Cut off the crown of leaves and trim the bottom end from the pineapple. Set the pineapple upright and pare off the skin with a small, sharp knife, cutting just below the surface in long, vertical strips and leaving the brown spots, or "eyes," on the fruit. Aligning the knife's blade with the rows of eyes, cut shallow furrows to remove them. Cut the pineapple in half lengthwise, then cut each half in half lengthwise. Cut two of the pineapple quarters into 4 thin wedges each, trimming away the fibrous core. Reserve the remaining pineapple for snacks or other uses.

Stand the mango on one of its narrowest ends. Cut the mango off-center, just grazing one side of the pit. Repeat on the other side. Score the cut side of each lobe lengthwise into 4 wedges, without piercing the peel. Press the mango lobes inside out and slice off the wedges of fruit near the peel.

Arrange the pineapple and mango wedges on 4 small dessert plates. In a small bowl, combine the lime juice, chili powder, and cayenne, if using. Spoon the spice mixture evenly over the fruit. Serve immediately, or cover and refrigerate for up to 30 minutes.

NUTRIENT ANALYSIS FOR ONE SERVING

Calories 65	**Calories from Carbs** 93%	**Total Fat** <1 g
Calories from Fat 3%	**Carbohydrates** 17 g	**Saturated Fat** 0 g
Protein 1 g	Fiber 2 g	**Monounsaturated Fat** 0 g
Cholesterol 0 mg	Sugars 13 g	**Polyunsaturated Fat** 0 g

BROILED NECTARINES

SODIUM PER SERVING

0 mg   daily limit 2300 mg

SERVES 4

If you are using your grill to cook dinner, you can set the dressed nectarines around the edges of the grill and cook them covered, just until tender, at the same time. You can substitute fresh peaches for the nectarines.

Preheat the broiler and position the broiler pan 4–6 inches from the heat.

Place the nectarines, cut side up, on a small baking sheet. Sprinkle the cinnamon and drizzle the honey over the nectarines. Broil until the nectarines are heated through and the honey is bubbly, 3–4 minutes. Transfer to small dessert dishes and garnish with the mint, if using.

2 large nectarines, halved and pitted

½ teaspoon ground cinnamon

1 tablespoon honey

4 teaspoons thinly sliced fresh mint (optional)

NUTRIENT ANALYSIS FOR ONE SERVING

Calories 53	**Calories from Carbs** 92%	**Total Fat** 0 g
Calories from Fat 4%	**Carbohydrates** 12 g	**Saturated Fat** 0 g
Protein 1 g	**Fiber** 1 g	**Monounsaturated Fat** 0 g
Cholesterol 0 mg	**Sugars** 10 g	**Polyunsaturated Fat** 0 g

6 g

YOGURT WITH WALNUTS & FIGS

SERVES 4

⅓ cup coarsely chopped walnuts

2 cups nonfat plain yogurt

½ cup diced dried figs

2 teaspoons honey or pure maple syrup

Dash of ground cinnamon or freshly ground nutmeg (optional)

This refreshing dessert showcases the savory-sweet flavors of toasted walnuts and dried figs. If dried figs are not available, substitute chopped dried dates.

Toast the walnuts according to the instructions on page 139.

Divide the yogurt among 4 small dessert bowls. Top with the toasted walnuts and dried figs. Drizzle the honey on top and garnish with the cinnamon, if using.

NUTRIENT ANALYSIS FOR ONE SERVING

Calories 189	**Calories from Carbs** 57%	**Total Fat** 6 g
Calories from Fat 28%	**Carbohydrates** 30 g	**Saturated Fat** 0 g
Protein 8 g	Fiber 4 g	**Monounsaturated Fat** 2 g
Cholesterol 3 mg	Sugars 26 g	**Polyunsaturated Fat** 4 g

CHOCOLATE-DIPPED APRICOTS

FAT COUNT

6g

SODIUM PER SERVING

5 mg   daily limit 2300 mg

SERVES 4

These richly elegant treats are ready in no time and make a satisfying dessert with a cup of coffee. Buy the best-quality chocolate you can find. To speed up the chocolate's setting, refrigerate the apricots for 15 minutes after dipping.

2 oz bittersweet chocolate, chopped (about ½ cup)

24 small dried apricots

Line a baking sheet with waxed paper.

Place the chocolate in a 1-cup glass measuring cup. Cook in a microwave oven at high power for 1 minute. Stir well and continue to microwave until the chocolate is melted, 20–30 seconds longer. Alternatively, place the chocolate in a very small saucepan or double boiler over low heat and cook, stirring often, until the chocolate is melted, 2–4 minutes. Remove from the heat.

Tilt the cup or saucepan and, using your fingers or tongs, dip an apricot three-fourths of the way into the chocolate. Scrape the excess chocolate from the back of the apricot and transfer to the waxed paper. Repeat with the remaining apricots and chocolate. Let the dipped apricots stand at room temperature until the chocolate sets, about 45 minutes. Serve immediately, or store in a tightly covered container at room temperature for up to 2 days.

NUTRIENT ANALYSIS FOR ONE SERVING

Calories 181	**Calories from Carbs** 67%	**Total Fat** 6 g
Calories from Fat 29%	**Carbohydrates** 32 g	**Saturated Fat** 3 g
Protein 2 g	**Fiber** 3 g	**Monounsaturated Fat** 1 g
Cholesterol 0 mg	**Sugars** 5 g	**Polyunsaturated Fat** 1 g

INGREDIENTS & TECHNIQUES

ARUGULA

Also known as rocket, this leafy salad green has a tangy, peppery taste. Its markedly notched leaves resemble elongated oak leaves and measure about 3 inches in length. Look for bunches with bright green leaves and no signs of wilting. Remove any thick stem ends before using. Arugula should be stored in a tightly sealed plastic bag in the refrigerator and used within a day or two.

CAPERS

The flower buds of a spiny Mediterranean shrub, capers have a pleasantly pungent flavor. They lend a bright piquancy to a wide variety of sauces, salads, and dips. Although they are commonly available pickled in vinegar, capers that have been packed in salt retain the best flavor and texture. Briefly soak pickled capers or rinse salted ones in cold water to remove excess salt before using.

BROWN RICE

Brown rice has not been processed by milling or polishing. Its brown hull is still intact, thus retaining the grain's fiber, B vitamins, minerals, and oils. Brown rice takes longer to cook than white rice, and has a chewier texture and more robust taste. Short-, medium-, and long-grain varieties are available. Store in an airtight container and use within 6 months, or within 1 year if refrigerated.

CHILES

A staple around the world, chiles—also known as hot peppers—vary in shape, color, flavor, and heat levels. Most ripen from green to bright red, sweetening as they redden. Popular and versatile jalapeños register medium to hot. Poblanos are larger, slightly milder, and dark green to red-brown in color. Roast them first to bring out their smoky, earthy flavor and then add them to soups, stews, and sauces.

CUMIN

Cumin has a sharp, strong flavor perfect for use in assertive dishes. The seeds of a member of the parsley family, cumin is available both ground and whole. For superior flavor, buy whole light-brown seeds and toast them before grinding for use as needed. All spices, including cumin, should be stored in tightly covered containers in a cool, dark place. They usually keep for up to 1 year.

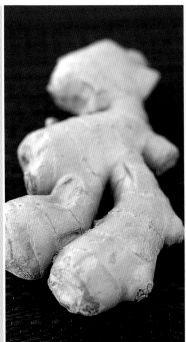

GINGER

Gnarled and knobby in appearance, ginger has a thin brown skin that is easy to remove with a knife or vegetable peeler. Fresh ginger has a refreshing and slightly sweet flavor that is also quite spicy. Select heavy pieces that are firm and smooth with slightly shiny skin. Store it unpeeled in a tightly sealed plastic bag in the refrigerator for up to 3 weeks or in the freezer for up to 1 year.

FETA

All cheeses are high in calcium and protein, but fat and sodium contents vary greatly. Feta cheese is low in fat but quite high in sodium, so it should be used in moderation. Traditionally made from sheep's milk, feta cheese can also be made from cow's or goat's milk. It is known for its crumbly, sometimes creamy texture. Reduced-fat and fat-free versions are also available.

HERBS

Choose fresh herbs that are fragrant and look bright and healthy. Avoid any that have wilted or discolored leaves. Fresh herbs should be refrigerated in sealed plastic bags. Buy dried herbs in small amounts and store them in tightly covered glass jars. Since dried herbs have more concentrated flavors, use one-fourth the amount of the fresh version called for in the recipe.

KALAMATA OLIVES

A popular variety from Greece, Kalamata olives are almond-shaped, purplish-black in color, and have a rich and meaty taste. They are usually brine-cured and then sold packed in oil or vinegar. When covered completely with water, brine, or oil, most olives will keep for up to 1 year in the refrigerator. Olives are rich in antioxidants, vitamins, and cholesterol-improving fats.

LEEKS

Leeks are the mildest-tasting member of the onion family, and, like onions and garlic, they are rich in potassium, which may help lower blood pressure. They should have bright white stalks and long, overlapping green leaves. Choose smaller leeks that have dark green tips and that are crisp, firm, and free of blemishes. Leeks will keep refrigerated in a sealed plastic bag for up to 5 days.

KALE & CHARD

Kale has firm, dark green, lightly crinkled leaves on long stems. This member of the cabbage family is rich in vitamins A and B, and the minerals calcium and iron. It retains its texture well when cooked. Chard, also called Swiss chard, has large, crinkled leaves on white stems. Red chard has red stalks and a more earthy flavor than the white kind, which tends to taste somewhat sweet.

LENTILS

A staple in the Middle East for 8,000 years, lentils are available in dozens of types grown around the world. Varieties include the common brown lentil found in most supermarkets, dark green Le Puy lentils from France, yellow lentils from India, and the small red lentils of Egypt. Although always sold dried, they do not require presoaking and cook to tenderness in only 20 to 30 minutes.

NUTMEG

Native to Indonesia, nutmeg has a warm, sweet-spicy flavor that marries well with spinach, fish, meat fillings, milk-based dishes, and many desserts. Because its aromatic oils dissipate quickly once the seed is ground, try to use whole nutmeg whenever possible. Although specially designed nutmeg graters ensure the finest shavings for cooking, any type of fine-holed grater will also work well.

PARMIGIANO-REGGIANO

This trademarked aged cow's-milk cheese is named for the Italian provinces of Parma and Reggio Emilia and is renowned for its complex and appealing flavor. As it tastes quite salty, a small amount can add great depth of taste to a dish, especially when the cheese is top quality, purchased in block form, and grated by hand just before serving.

OLIVE OIL

Essential to Mediterranean cuisine, olive oils can be bright green and peppery or mellow gold and slightly sweet. Extra-virgin olive oil, the highest-quality grade, retains the most color and flavor, but it is best reserved for sauces and quick sautés, as it loses character at even moderate temperatures. Regular olive oil, lighter in flavor and color, holds up well to high-heat cooking such as frying.

SESAME OIL

Made from toasted sesame seeds, dark sesame oil has a rich amber color and an intense, nutty flavor. Clear, refined sesame oils are better for high-heat cooking, but dark oils offer more flavor, even in tiny amounts. Look for them in Asian markets or the ethnic or international aisle of supermarkets. More perishable than other oils, dark sesame oil is best stored in the refrigerator.

SHALLOTS

Diminutive members of the onion family, shallots grow in small clusters much like garlic. Their papery reddish-brown skin covers white flesh tinged with pink or purple. Although layered like onions, with a similar pungent aroma, they are valued for their more delicate flavor, which is particularly good in sauces and vinaigrettes. Store shallots in a cool, dark place with good air circulation.

SUN-DRIED TOMATOES

Dehydrated plum tomatoes are sold dried (labeled "dry-packed") or packed in oil. Dry-packed tomatoes must be soaked for 5 minutes in hot water before using. They contain almost no fat (compared with the oil-packed variety), and they are naturally low in calories and sodium. All tomatoes are rich in the antioxidant vitamins A and C as well as lycopene.

SPECIALTY VINEGARS

From the French for "sour wine," vinegar forms when bacteria turn a fermented liquid into a weak solution of acetic acid. Red wine, white wine, balsamic, and sherry vinegars are among the best for cooking, as they display traits of the wines from which they are made, along with a sourness that makes them valuable in balancing flavors. Look for top-quality, unfiltered aged vinegars.

SWEET POTATOES

Although often confused with yams, sweet potatoes have a sweeter taste and less starchy flesh. They are excellent baked whole, roasted or braised with a honey or maple syrup glaze, or mashed with a touch of cinnamon or nutmeg. Store in a cool, dark, well-ventilated place but avoid refrigerating them, as cold temperatures will alter their flavor.

TOASTING NUTS

Cooking nuts until they are golden deepens their flavor and improves their texture. You can toast nuts by baking them on a cookie sheet in a 325°F oven or by stirring them in a small, dry, nonstick frying pan over medium-high heat. Cook them just until they're fragrant and golden in color, about 5–10 minutes. Take care not to overcook them, as they will become bitter when scorched.

WHEAT BRAN & WHEAT GERM

During the milling of wheat, the kernel's outer covering, known as the bran, and its tiny embryo, the germ, are usually both removed. Sold in health-food stores and most supermarkets, wheat bran and wheat germ add nutrient value to cereals, casseroles, fillings, and baked goods. Unless the germ is defatted, it should be stored in an airtight container in the refrigerator.

TOFU

Soy milk, made from cooked soybeans, forms tofu when curdled and pressed into blocks. Although bland, plain tofu readily absorbs flavors from marinades and sauces. The smooth texture of silken tofu is ideal for soups and for puréeing. Firm tofu, denser and coarser in texture, holds together well for stir-frying and grilling. To store tofu, submerge it in cold water and refrigerate.

ZEST

The thin outer peel of citrus fruits, known as the zest, is rich in aromatic oils. Any fine-holed grater will shred the zest into delicate shavings that are perfect for marinades or rubs. You can also use a zester to create thin, elegant strips for garnish. Do not cut or grate into the white, pulpy pith just beneath the outer peel, as it has a spongy texture and an unpleasantly bitter flavor.

INDEX

MEREDITH® BOOKS

Publisher and Editor in Chief: James D. Blume

Executive Director, Marketing: Jeffrey Myers
Editorial Director: Linda Raglan Cunningham
Executive Director, New Business Development: Todd M. Davis
Executive Director, Sales: Ken Zagor
Director, Operations: George A. Susral
Director, Production: Douglas M. Johnston
Business Director: Jim Leonard

Vice President and General Manager: Douglas J. Guendel

Meredith Publishing Group
President, Publishing Group: Stephen M. Lacy
Vice President–Publishing Director: Bob Mate

Meredith Corporation
Chairman and Chief Executive Officer: William T. Kerr

In Memoriam: E.T. Meredith III (1933–2003)

AMERICAN MEDICAL ASSOCIATION

Executive Vice President,
    Chief Executive Officer: Michael D. Maves, M.D., M.B.A.
Senior Vice President,
    Publishing and Business Services: Robert A. Musacchio, Ph.D.
Vice President, Business Products: Anthony J. Frankos
Chief Operations Officer, AMA Press: Mary Lou White
Managing Editor: Donna Kotulak
Art Editor: Mary Ann Albanese
Medical Editor: Bonnie Chi-Lum, M.D., M.P.H.
Contributing Editor: Maryellen Westerberg, Dr.P.H., R.D., C.D.E.

The recommendations and information in this book are appropriate in most cases and current as of the date of publication. For specific information concerning your or a family member's medical condition, the AMA suggests that you consult a physician.

WELDON OWEN INC.

Chief Executive Officer: John Owen
President and Chief Operating Officer: Terry Newell
Chief Financial Officer: Christine E. Munson
Vice President International Sales: Stuart Laurence
Creative Director: Gaye Allen
Associate Publisher: Val Cipollone
Editor: Emily Miller
Contributing Editor: Sheridan Warrick
Designer: Leon Yu
Editorial Assistant: Juli Vendzules
Copy Editor: Carrie Bradley
Proofreaders: Arin Hailey and Sharron Wood
Indexer: Ken DellaPenta
Production Director: Chris Hemesath
Color Manager: Teri Bell
Production and Reprint Coordinator: Todd Rechner

The American Medical Association Hypertension Cookbook
Conceived and produced by Weldon Owen Inc.
814 Montgomery Street, San Francisco, CA 94133
Telephone: 415-291-0100 Fax: 415-291-8841

First printed in 2005
10 9 8 7 6 5 4 3 2 1

ISBN: 0-696-22443-7
Printed by Midas Printing Limited, China

Acknowledgments
Thanks to Nicky Collings, Joan Olsen, and Colin Wheatland for design assistance; Kim Konecny and Erin Quon for food styling; Leigh Noë for prop styling; and Selena Aument and Guarina Lopez for assisting in the studio.

Photographs by Jim Franco: page 11, page 12 (three at bottom), page 13 (three at top right corner), page 14 (three at top left corner), page 16 (three at top left corner), page 17, page 19, page 134 (top and bottom right), page 136 (bottom right), page 137 (top and bottom left, bottom right), page 138 (top and bottom left, bottom right), page 139.